FOOTBALL FACTS FOR CURIOUS FANS

HAYDEN FOX

Parents,
Claim Your Free Gifts!

Simply visit **haydenfoxmedia.com** to receive the following:

- *1000 Conversation Starters the Whole Family Will Love*

- *100 Fun Screen-Free Activity Ideas to Enjoy Together as a Family*

(you can also scan this QR code)

Chapter 1: History Facts

1. Originally performed primarily in prestigious American colleges in the late 19th century, American football started as a mix of soccer and rugby.

19th century

2. On November 6, 1869, Rutgers and Princeton participated in the first intercollegiate football game, considered a precursor to American football.

Rutgers
Vs
Princeton

3. The rules used in the 1869 Rutgers and Princeton games were a mix of soccer and rugby and prohibited forward passing.

4. Known as the "Father of American Football," Walter Camp instituted late 1870s regulations, including the snap and the line of scrimmage.

5. Founded in 1876, the Intercollegiate Football Association established early rules for the emerging sport of American football.

6. In early American football, field goals were worth more points than touchdowns until 1912, when the scoring system was rebalanced.

7. Athletes originally wore simple clothing without protective gear but leather helmets were introduced in the early 1900s.

1900

8. Reacting to a marked increase in injuries and deaths, President Theodore Roosevelt campaigned in 1905 for more sensible football regulations.

9. In 1906, the NCAA was founded in response to calls for reform, overseeing college football and promoting player safety.

. Approved as a rule change in 1906 to
educe injuries, the forward pass marked a
major shift in the game's strategy.

. Until the middle of the 20th century,
college football far outstripped
professional football in popularity.

12. Early professional
football started with
autonomous clubs, mostly
composed of athletic
organizations not yet
affiliated into any formal
league.

3. In 1892, Pudge Heffelfinger became
the first known professional football
player when he was paid $500 to play
or the Allegheny Athletic Association.

14. Professional football leagues began to
appear in Pennsylvania around 1898 and
gained popularity in the early 1900s as
teams started paying players.

15. The Ohio League was one of the first
regional associations of professional
football teams, though it lacked a national
structure.

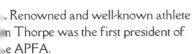

1
8
9
2

$500

. Established in 1920, the American
Professional Football Association
(APFA) adopted the NFL
(National Football League) name in
22.

06

18. Early APFA teams were
mainly based in Ohio, Illinois,
Indiana, and nearby states,
including New York, reflecting
the Midwest roots of professional
football.

. Renowned and well-known athlete
Jim Thorpe was the first president of
the APFA.

. One of the first games under the APFA,
which would later become the NFL, took
place on October 3, 1920, with the Dayton
Triangles defeating the Columbus
Panhandles.

. The NFL adopted a uniform
championship game to ascertain the
best team of the season in 1933.

21. The forward pass became ever more
crucial as teams created more intricate
passing techniques in the 1930s.

22. The NFL suffered from poor attendance and
financial issues in its early years even as it
survived the Great Depression.

23. In 1936, the NFL held its first ever draft.

24. Beginning the NFL's television coverage in 1939, the first game shown between the Philadelphia Eagles and the Brooklyn Dodgers started off the program.

25. In 1939, the NFL held an All-Star Game featuring top players; the official Pro Bowl began in 1951.

26. The NFL adopted sudden death overtime for championship games in 1946.

Championship games

1946

27. World War II significantly influenced the NFL; some players were selected for service, and several clubs temporarily combined to cover their rosters.

28. The All-America Football Conference (AAFC) was a rival professional league from 1946 to 1949; it then merged with the NFL.

29. The NFL merger in 1949 included clubs from the AAFC, such as the Cleveland Browns.

31. The 1958 NFL Championship Game between the Baltimore Colts and New York Giants became the first to use sudden-death overtime after the game ended in a tie.

30. In 1950, the NFL split into two divisions—American and National—in order to incorporate new AAFC clubs.

32. The 1958 Championship Game is widely credited with helping to popularize professional football across the United States.

33. By the 1960s, television broadcasts and expanded market reach helped the NFL begin to surpass Major League Baseball in popularity.

34. In 1960, the American Football League (AFL) emerged as a competitor to the NFL and introduced innovations like the two-point conversion.

35. The AFL gained recognition with high-profile events, competitive salaries, and a television deal with ABC.

36. The first Super Bowl, held in 1967, featured the champions of the NFL and AFL and evolved into the NFL's annual championship game.

37. The NFL and AFL officially merged in 1970 to form a single league with two conferences: the NFC and AFC.

38. Monday Night Football became the first major sports program to air in primetime when it debuted in 1970.

39. By scheduling games on Thanksgiving Day starting in 1971, the NFL revived an early 20th-century tradition.

40. In the 1970s, the NFL expanded to 26 teams, establishing a nationwide franchise network.

41. In 1978, the NFL expanded the regular season to 16 games to increase revenue and fan engagement.

42. Founded in 1982, the NFL Scouting Combine became a significant event for evaluating college prospects.

43. During the first major league strike in 1982, the NFL Players' Association reduced the season to nine games over 57 days.

44. The 1987 players' strike shortened the season and led to three weeks of games played with replacement players.

45. .First tested in the 1980s, instant replay returned in 1999 after technology improvements and debates over close calls.

46.In the 1990s, the NFL expanded internationally, hosting games in Mexico, Tokyo, and London as part of the American Bowl series.

47. Founded in 1991 as the World League of American Football and later rebranded as NFL Europe in 1998, the league operated as a developmental program until 2007 to popularize American football across Europe.

48. The 1994 salary cap aimed to balance financial resources across teams and prevent wealthier teams from dominating talent acquisition.

49. The 2002 'tuck rule' game between the Patriots and Raiders brought significant attention to the existing rule, leading to further league review.

50. Introduced in 2003, the NFL's Rooney Rule requires teams to interview minority candidates for head coaching positions.

51. The NFL's first global broadcast, Super Bowl XXXIX 2005, reached over 230 countries.

52. The NFL launched the International Series in 2007, starting with regular-season games held at London's Wembley Stadium.

London's Wembley Stadium

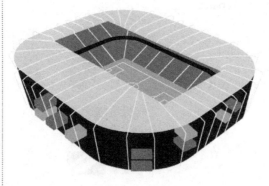

53. In 2010, the NFL changed its overtime rules for the postseason to ensure each team has an opportunity to possess the ball.

54. The NFL's 2011 labor lockout resulted in a new collective bargaining agreement strengthening player safety protocols.

55. In the early 2010s, the NFL began implementing stricter player safety regulations regarding concussions and head injuries.

56. In 2020, the NFL modified its playoff structure to include 14 teams, adding one extra wild card slot per conference.

57. .After switching to a 16-game season in 1978, the NFL made its only other schedule change in 2021 by adding a 17th regular-season game.

58. .Katie Sowers became the first woman to coach in a Super Bowl, assisting at Super Bowl LIV in 2020.

59. Established to honor players, coaches, and contributors, the Pro Football Hall of Fame opened in Canton, Ohio 1963.

60. With the Super Bowl often ranking as the most-watched annual sporting event in the U.S., the NFL has become the most-watched sports league in the country.

Chapter 2: Broadcasting Facts

1. Originally performed primarily in prestigious American colleges in the late 19th century, American football started as a mix of soccer and rugby.1."Sunday Night Football" is the most-watched TV show in the United States during the fall.

2. The NFL documentary series "Hard Knocks" gives viewers an up-close look at a team during training camp.

NFL Documentary

5.Many NFL events are now available in 4K, offering visuals with enhanced depth and clarity.

6. NBC was the first network to air the Super Bowl in color, starting with Super Bowl IV in 1970.

3. NFL broadcasts frequently include "mic'd up" segments, providing viewers insight into player interactions throughout the game.

4. Each Super Bowl features a unique logo that often becomes iconic and is highly sought after by fans.

7.The NFL relies on advanced data and analytics to enhance viewer understanding of the game.

8.NFL broadcasts often emphasize player health and safety, focusing on issues like concussions.

9. The NFL broadcasts are known for sophisticated pre-game programming, blending interviews, analysis, and expert commentary.

10. Major networks engage in intense bidding wars for the highly coveted NFL broadcasting rights.

11. NFL broadcasts often feature guest experts, including former players and coaches, to provide additional insights.

12. Many NFL games are broadcast internationally with various commentary teams and formats to appeal to a global audience.

13. Super Bowl commercials are widely anticipated and frequently discussed in the days leading up to the game.

14. NFL broadcasts frequently highlight key player statistics and career achievements to enhance viewer appreciation of players' skills.

15. NFL broadcasts sometimes include real-time tracking statistics, displaying multiple game events as they happen.

16. Weather delays can significantly impact broadcast plans and game preparations, requiring flexibility from broadcasters.

17. Since 2015, the NFL's "Next Gen Stats" has provided real-time player tracking data for every game, enhancing fan experience.

18. NFL broadcasts often include on-field interviews with players and coaches at halftime, offering direct insights into game strategies.

19. Many NFL broadcasters have personal experience as former professional athletes, adding depth to their commentary.

20. Some broadcasters use advanced analytics to enhance the quality of their game commentary and analysis.

21. Pre-game and halftime shows in NFL broadcasts often emphasize key narratives, building excitement and anticipation for viewers.

22. NFL broadcasts often include well-known guest analysts and commentators to provide diverse perspectives on the game.

23. The increasing number of female reporters and analysts adds diversity to NFL broadcasting perspectives.

24. NFL broadcasts usually feature local production crews for each team, providing a tailored experience for regional fans.

25. Celebrities like Conan O'Brien and Jimmy Fallon have hosted NFL events, adding entertainment value to the broadcasts.

NFL Events

26. Many NFL broadcasts include sideline access during timeouts, allowing viewers a closer look at player and coach interactions.

27. The NFL frequently airs games in multiple languages to cater to a diverse, global audience.

28. NFL broadcasts often incorporate player health initiatives and provide awareness about player safety, particularly around head injuries.

29. The 'All-22' camera view enhances coaches' and analysts' ability to examine player formations from various angles.

30. Trademark restrictions around 'Super Bowl' in advertising have led to the game being referred to as the 'Big Game.'

31. Initially gaining popularity in the 1970s, the "Game of the Week" highlighted the most exciting matchups.

32. Along with replays and condensed versions, the 'Game Pass' subscription lets fans watch all NFL games live.

33. The "Hail Mary" play became a significant highlight during broadcasts in the 1970s.

34. HBO's 'Hard Knocks' series provides viewers an inside look at one NFL team's players and coaches each preseason.

35. The "Last Two Minutes" rule requires careful analysis during crucial game-changing moments.

36. Peyton and Eli Manning's "Manningcast" gained popularity for its relaxed approach to Monday Night Football analysis.

7. The "Pass Interference Challenge" was a minor attempt to improve officiating during broadcasts.

8. Viewers of the "Red Zone Channel" can watch multiple games and highlights in real-time simultaneously.

9. The "Red Zone" channel alerts viewers to potential scoring opportunities during Sunday games.

10. "SkyCam" technology provides special overhead views that enhance the game viewing experience.

11. The "Telestrator," originally designed for video marking, became well-known during NFL broadcasts in the 1980s.

12. The NFL season now prominently features the "Thursday Night Football" package.

13. The "Two-Minute Warning" is particularly significant and generates excitement at the end of each half.

14. An NFL game in 2020, which lasted approximately three hours and twelve minutes, marked the first broadcast featuring an all-female commentary team.

15. NFL draft telecasts first began in 1980.

NFL

Telecast

1

9

8

0

46. The first NFL game ever broadcast on television was between the Brooklyn Dodgers and the Philadelphia Eagles in 1939.

47. Nearly 60 million people watched the inaugural Super Bowl in 1967.

48. The Super Bowl halftime show often contrasts with the game regarding audience engagement and production quality.

49. Super Bowl XLIX in 2015 became the most-watched event in U.S. television history at that time, with approximately 114.4 million viewers.

50. The NFL has embraced social media integration to help viewers connect with the league.

51. New technologies developed by the league aim to reduce officiating errors during broadcasts.

52. The NFL has made progress in providing diverse perspectives in-game analysis.

53. The league often collaborates with companies to create immersive advertising experiences for TV shows.

54. NFL broadcasts frequently feature player stories and personal histories to strengthen emotional connections with viewers.

55. Today, the NFL Draft is a major television event with celebrity participation and red-carpet appearances.

56. The NFL employs a variety of professional analysts, each specializing in different aspects of the game.

57. The NFL has facilitated the growth of the "fantasy football" trend through its broadcasts.

58. To enhance the viewer experience, the NFL has developed various smartphone apps.

59. Virtual reality technology provides fans with immersive viewing experiences offered by the NFL.

60. The NFL has increased its presence on streaming platforms to engage younger audiences.

61. The NFL has explored first-person view perspectives using player-mounted cameras among its various camera angles.

62. The league maintains a dedicated radio network for live game coverage and commentary.

63. The official NFL YouTube channel features an abundance of highlights and analysis.

64. The NFL has initiated programs to boost diversity in sports media and broadcasting.

65. The league aims to increase TV coverage for people with disabilities.

66. The NFL has sought to showcase global stories and international athletes throughout its events.

67. The NFL has partnered with various technology companies to enhance the augmented-reality viewing experience.

68. The NFL has affiliations with several networks, including ESPN, CBS, FOX, and NBC.

69. The NFL strives to provide complete coverage for fans across various time zones.

70. Originally launched in 2003, the NFL Network offers continuous league coverage year-round.

71. The NFL employs multiple camera crews for every game to capture every viewpoint and action.

72. Teams have shared revenue from broadcasting rights based on their official NFL television contracts since 1961.

73. With millions of fans on platforms like Twitter, Instagram, and TikTok, the NFL is highly active on social media.

74. NFL games often spark discussions about the value of strong defense, emphasizing the idea that its importance can't be easily quantified.

75. The Super Bowl halftime performance, usually featuring A-list musicians, is considered the most significant musical event of the year.

76. The Super Bowl consistently ranks among the most-watched TV events in the U.S., attracting around 90-100 million viewers.

77. The Super Bowl is regarded as a sporting event with cultural significance comparable to major American cultural events.

78. Typically viewed as the most expensive television advertising opportunity, a 30-second commercial during the Super Bowl costs around $5 million.

79. Originally aired in 1970, "Monday Night Football" transformed sports television.

80. Incorporating analytics into broadcasts helps viewers comprehend game strategies more effectively.

81. Another perspective on gameplay is provided by "helmet cameras," which offer a player's vantage point.

82. Modern microphones have enhanced broadcast audio quality by effectively capturing ambient crowd noise and player interactions.

83. Animated player models improve the presentation of plays more engagingly.

84. Today, NFL events feature increased aerial footage captured by drones.

85. Visuals and animations clarify complex gestures and techniques during broadcasts.

86. Released by the Chicago Bears in 1985, the 'Super Bowl Shuffle' became one of the first songs closely associated with an NFL team.

87. Remarkable calls made by announcers have significantly influenced the history of the NFL.

88. The league continuously adapts its broadcasting style to align with changing consumer preferences.

89. Through virtual reality experiences, several games allow fans to feel genuinely part of the action from their homes.

90. The NFL has launched educational initiatives through broadcast channels to engage viewers with the game.

91. The increasing collaboration between the NFL and significant networks reflects the league's growing popularity.

92. The league adjusts its broadcasting schedule each NFL season to maintain public interest and entertainment value.

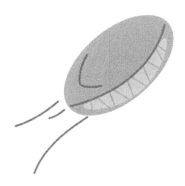

Chapter 3: Season and Postseason

1. The NFL season includes the regular season, playoffs, and culminates in the Super Bowl.

2. The league comprises thirty-two teams organized into the American Football Conference (AFC) and the National Football Conference (NFC).

3. Each conference has four divisions containing four teams: North, South, East, and West.

4. Starting in 2021, the regular season was extended from 16 to 17 games.

5. Each team has one "bye week" during the regular season for rest and recovery.

6. The NFL scheduling ensures that once every four years, each team plays against every other team through a rotating schedule.

7. The NFL regular season runs from September to January, while the playoffs occur in January and February.

8. Teams play each divisional opponent twice per season, totaling six games—once at home and once away.

9. Each team plays four games against teams from another division within their conference, with divisions changing annually.

10. Teams play four games against a division from the opposite conference in alternating years.

11. Each team plays three "strength of schedule" games against teams from the other divisions in their conference based on their performance from the previous year.

2. Each conference consists of 16 teams, with seven from each conference qualifying for the playoffs, totaling 14 teams.

3. The top seed in each conference receives a first-round bye in the playoffs, advancing directly to the Divisional Round.

14. The NFL playoffs follow a single-elimination format, meaning each game determines whether a team advances to the next round.

5. In each conference, the second seed plays the seventh seed in the Wild Card Round, the third seed faces the sixth seed, and the fourth seed plays the fifth seed.

16. Following a reseeding pattern, the top remaining seed in each conference faces the lowest remaining seed in the Divisional Round.

17. The AFC and NFC champions typically compete at a neutral site on the second Sunday of February in the Super Bowl.

8. The NFL expanded its playoff system twice—from 10 teams to 12 in 1990, and from 12 to 14 in 2020.

9. Teams from the same division can face each other in the playoffs, including the conference championship game.

20. Except for the Super Bowl, home-field advantage belongs to the team with the better seed.

21. Home-field advantage in the playoffs is significant, as home teams generally have a better-winning record.

22. Held initially after the Super Bowl, the Pro Bowl is an all-star game for the NFL's top players, now scheduled for the week prior.

23. During the playoffs, the NFL tested a "sudden death" rule, which led to the current overtime system, allowing each team a chance to possess the ball.

24. The strength of each NFL team's schedule is determined by their previous season's win-loss record.

25. The NFL Draft order is determined by each team's regular-season performance, with the team having the worst record selecting first.

26. The AFC and NFC conferences, originally autonomous leagues, came together in 1970 to create the modern NFL structure.

AFC and NFC

1970

NFL

27. Each game begins with a coin toss to determine possession.

28. Wild Card Weekend typically features two games each on Saturday and Sunday.

29. The Divisional Round and Conference Championships occur after Wild Card Weekend, determining the final playoff teams.

30. Each year, teams are scheduled to play other teams from their conference that finished in the same position in their respective divisions, fostering competition.

31. The Super Bowl cannot be hosted by any NFL franchise in consecutive seasons.

32. During the last seven weeks of the regular season, the NFL uses its "flexible scheduling" tool to move major events to prime time.

33. Since 1934, Thanksgiving Day games have been an NFL tradition, always featuring at least one game between the Detroit Lions and the Dallas Cowboys.

34. At least one team with a losing record has qualified for the playoffs since the 2020 expansion, most notably exemplified by the NFC East winner advancing with a 7-9 record.

35. The NFL's 'season finale' features games between divisional rivals to heighten drama and postseason stakes.

36. To support the NFL's international following, every team must play at least one game abroad every eight years.

37. Events on the NFL calendar include "Thursday Night Football," which provides fans with additional weekly NFL content.

8. The NFC East is the only division in which every team has won the Super Bowl at least once, achieving championship glory.

9. NFL divisions can vary significantly in competitiveness; "wild card" teams may have better records than division champions.

0. Every division has had four teams since 2002, maintaining competitive balance and consistency in division size.

4 Teams

41. The "bye week," established in 1990, provides teams with a mid-season break.

42. The NFL initially planned for a single-bye schedule but experimented with a double-bye season in 1993, allowing each team two byes.

43. A division clinch guarantees a home playoff game, regardless of whether a team has a worse record than a wild card team.

44. Unlike other American sports leagues, the NFL reseeds teams after every playoff round.

45. NFL players wear specific patches and decals to indicate their participation in postseason rounds, including the AFC and NFC Championship marks.

46. The Super Bowl is scheduled in February, partly to accommodate any regular-season games rescheduled due to weather delays.

America Sports League

47. The NFL prohibits teams from "tanking" for draft picks; actions suggesting deliberate failure can result in fines or penalties.

48. The NFL's salary cap limits the total amount each team can spend on player compensation, promoting equity within the league.

49. Only three teams with losing records have reached the playoffs throughout NFL history, each winning their division despite a poor season.

50. Each team's regular season schedule includes intra-conference, divisional, and inter-conference games.

51. The Super Bowl location alternates yearly between domed and warm-weather sites.

52. The NFL divisions have undergone several changes, with the most recent adjustment occurring in 2002 when the Houston Texans joined as an expansion team.

53. To increase drama and postseason significance, the regular season's penultimate week consists solely of divisional games.

54. The NFL hosts a "London Series," featuring several games at Tottenham Hotspur Stadium or Wembley.

55. At the end of the season, every team receives a conference ranking from 1 to 7 that determines playoff seeding.

56. Fans, coaches, and players each contribute one-third of the vote in selecting the Pro Bowl rosters.

57. The top seed in each conference receives one 'bye' week, allowing them to skip the Wild Card round and proceed directly to the Divisional round.

58. The league's balance is evident as at least four teams that made the playoffs each year did not qualify the previous year.

59. NFL teams do not play against every other team every season; instead, they methodically rotate through inter-conference matchups every four years.

60. Despite having worse records, division champions receive higher playoff seeding than wild card teams.

61. Teams generally need 9-10 wins to qualify for the playoffs, although divisional rankings can sometimes allow lower-win teams to qualify.

62. The halftime entertainment and commercials significantly influence how the league engages a larger, potentially non-sporting audience.

63. The Super Bowl is a unique event, as the NFL is the only major sports league with neutral venues for its championship game.

Chapter 4: Notable Drafts

1. Using a pool of 90 eligible players, the Philadelphia Eagles hosted the first NFL Draft on February 8, 1936.

2. The first overall pick for the Philadelphia Eagles in the 1936 Draft was Jay Berwanger from the University of Chicago.

3. John Elway, Jim Kelly, and Dan Marino were three of the six future Pro Football Hall of Famers to emerge from the 1983 NFL Draft.

4. John Elway was selected first overall in the 1983 Draft by the Baltimore Colts, but he was traded to the Denver Broncos before ever playing for the Colts.

5. Peyton Manning, a future Hall of Famer, was the first overall pick by the Indianapolis Colts in the 1998 NFL Draft.

6. Randy Moss, selected 21st overall by the Minnesota Vikings, is considered one of the most gifted wide receivers in NFL history.

7. Eli Manning was selected first overall by the San Diego Chargers in the 2004 NFL Draft but was traded to the New York Giants shortly afterward.

8. The Pittsburgh Steelers selected Ben Roethlisberger as the 11th overall pick in the 2004 Draft, where he would later become one of the league's greatest quarterbacks.

9. It was remarkable when the Cleveland Browns chose Baker Mayfield as their first overall pick in the 2018 NFL Draft.

). Saquon Barkley, a running back from 'enn State, was the second overall pick nade by the New York Giants in the 2018 NFL Draft.

. The Carolina Panthers selected 'am Newton as the first overall pick n the 2011 NFL Draft, marking the start of his brilliant career.

12. In the first round of the 1985 Draft, the San Francisco 49ers selected Jerry Rice with the 16th overall pick, who would become one of the top wide receivers in NFL history.

3. Tiki Barber and Marvin Harrison both ntered the 1996 NFL Draft, with the ndianapolis Colts selecting Harrison 19th verall.

14. Peyton Manning and Ryan Leaf were notable members of the 1998 NFL Draft, often referred to as the "Great Quarterback Class."

15. Selected in the sixth round by the New England Patriots, Tom Brady was the 199th overall pick in the 2000 NFL Draft.

16. Larry Fitzgerald was chosen third overall by the Arizona Cardinals in the 2004 Draft and has had an outstanding career.

17. The 1989 NFL Draft is memorable because Troy Aikman was selected first overall by the Dallas Cowboys.

18. Deion Sanders was the fifth overall pick in the 1989 Draft by the Atlanta Falcons and is regarded as one of the finest cornerbacks in NFL history.

. Joe Montana was chosen by the San rancisco 49ers as the 82nd overall pick in e third round of the NFL Draft.

. The Atlanta Falcons' selection of ett Favre in the second round (33rd erall) of the NFL Draft made it an forgettable event.

21. Russell Wilson became a Super Bowl champion after being selected by the Seattle Seahawks in the third round (75th overall) of the Draft.

22. Facing backlash for their choice, the Chicago Bears selected Mitch Trubisky second overall in the 2017 NFL Draft.

23. EJ Manuel was selected as the first quarterback in the 2013 NFL Draft with the Buffalo Bills' 16th overall pick.

24. The Green Bay Packers later chose Hall of Famer and Super Bowl MVP Aaron Rodgers 24th overall in the 2005 NFL Draft.

25. Dan Marino, selected 27th overall by the Miami Dolphins, became one of the most successful quarterbacks from the 1983 NFL Draft.

26. Despite winning the Heisman Trophy, Johnny Manziel was selected 22nd overall by the Cleveland Browns in the 2014 NFL Draft.

27. Reggie Bush was selected second overall by the New Orleans Saints in the 2006 NFL Draft, marking it as an exceptional year.

28. Jim Plunkett was the first overall selection in the 1971 NFL Draft by the New England Patriots and later led the Raiders to two Super Bowl victories.

29. The 2009 NFL Draft highlighted quarterbacks like Matthew Stafford (first overall), Mark Sanchez (fifth), and Josh Freeman (17th).

31. T Michael Vick, selected first overall by the Atlanta Falcons in 2001, has been a revolutionary athlete in the NFL Draft's history.

30. Among prospects like Aaron Rodgers, Alex Smith was selected first overall by the San Francisco 49ers in the 2005 NFL Draft.

32. John Riggins was the sixth overall choice for the New York Jets in the 1973 NFL Draft, later becoming a Hall of Fame running back.

33. Marvin Harrison, selected in the 1996 NFL Draft, proved one of the league's top receivers in history.

34. Jared Goff was selected first overall in the Los Angeles Rams' 2016 NFL Draft, marking the beginning of a new chapter for the franchise.

35. Among several notable players from the 2002 NFL Draft, two noteworthy selections were Joey Harrington (third overall) and David Carr (first overall).

36. Matt Ryan, originally chosen third overall by the Atlanta Falcons in the 2008 NFL Draft, has become a franchise cornerstone.

37. The San Diego Chargers selected future Hall of Famer LaDainian Tomlinson with the fifth overall pick in the 2001 NFL Draft.

38. Herschel Walker joined the Dallas Cowboys in 1986 after his time in the USFL, bringing his explosive playing style to the NFL.

39. Steve McNair, chosen third overall by the Houston Oilers in the 1992 NFL Draft, had an outstanding career.

1992 NFL

40. The 1983 NFL Draft was significant for John Elway, who became a Hall of Fame inductee and Super Bowl champion.

41. Originally selected in the 1991 NFL Draft, Brett Favre enjoyed an extraordinary career that ultimately earned him a place in the Hall of Fame.

42. The Arizona Cardinals' first overall pick in the 2019 NFL Draft was Kyler Murray, who won the Heisman Trophy.

43. Carson Palmer, selected first overall by the Cincinnati Bengals in the 2003 NFL Draft, became a Pro Bowl quarterback.

44. JaMarcus Russell, a prominent player from the 2007 NFL Draft, disappointed the league after being selected first overall by the Oakland Raiders.

45. Tony Dorsett, a future Hall of Fame member, was the second overall choice of the Dallas Cowboys in the 1975 NFL Draft.

46. Eric Dickerson, selected second overall by the Los Angeles Rams in the 1982 NFL Draft, proved to be an exceptional running back.

47. Tyler Lockett, selected in the third round (69th overall), has been a valuable asset for the Seattle Seahawks.

48. Derrick Thomas, a Hall of Fame linebacker selected fourth overall by the Kansas City Chiefs in the 1990 NFL Draft, is particularly noteworthy.

49. The Arizona Cardinals selected Larry Fitzgerald third overall in the 2004 NFL Draft, and he went on to have an impressive career.

50. DeMarcus Ware was selected 11th overall by the Dallas Cowboys in the 2005 NFL Draft and has become an outstanding pass rusher.

51. Roger Staubach was selected in the tenth round of the 1972 NFL Draft and developed into an exceptional quarterback for the Dallas Cowboys.

52. The Pittsburgh Steelers chose Troy Polamalu with the 16th overall pick in the 2003 NFL Draft, making him a key player for the team.

53. Jeff George was selected first overall by the Indianapolis Colts in the 1990 NFL Draft and became known for his strong arm, though his career was inconsistent.

54. Keyshawn Johnson, chosen first by the New York Jets in the 1996 NFL Draft, had a remarkable career.

55. LaDainian Tomlinson, selected fifth overall by the San Diego Chargers, became a Hall of Fame inductee.

56. Joe Theismann, a standout quarterback for the Washington Redskins, was originally selected by the Miami Dolphins in the 1971 NFL Draft before making his mark in the NFL.

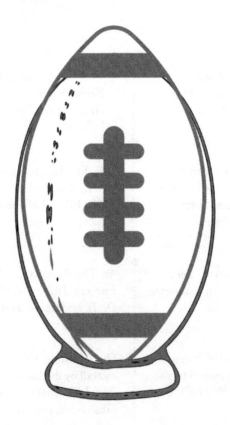

Chapter 5: Rules and Regulations

1. Every American football team has four downs to advance the ball ten yards. Once successful, they earn a new set of downs.

2. An American football field measures 120 yards in total, consisting of a 100-yard playing area and two 10-yard end zones.

3. In college football, teams have 25 seconds to snap the ball after it's set, while the NFL uses a 40-second play clock between plays.

4. A field goal is worth three points, while a touchdown—the primary objective in football—earns six points.

7. Regular season NFL overtime lasts ten minutes, while postseason overtime extends to fifteen minutes.

5. Teams can opt for a two-point conversion after a touchdown or a one-point conversion by kicking the ball through the uprights.

8. The NFL modified its overtime rules in 2012, stipulating that if the first team scores only a field goal, both teams will have a chance to possess the ball.

6. Introduced in 1994, the two-point conversion enhances scoring variability and strategic decision-making.

9. The NFL prohibits intentional forward passes after crossing the line of scrimmage, affecting both yardage and down counts.

10. A quarterback can "spike" the ball at the snap to stop the clock without violating any rules.

11. If the offense fails to snap the ball before the play clock expires, a "Delay of Game" penalty results in a five-yard loss.

12. American football allows one forward pass per play; any subsequent pass incurs a penalty.

13. The defense gains possession when a quarterback throws an interception, shifting the game's momentum.

14. In college football, pass interference penalties occur when a player obstructs an opponent's ability to receive the ball; in the NFL, these result in a spot-of-foul penalty.

15. Defensive players must line up at least one yard behind the line of scrimmage to avoid encroachment penalties.

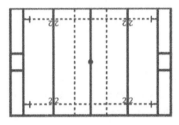

16. Offensive linemen cannot cross the line of scrimmage until the ball is snapped.

17. Forward passes thrown by offensive linemen result in penalties for ineligible receivers.

18. Only the quarterback and the backs are allowed to throw the ball; offensive linemeln are responsible only for blocking.

19. If the offense is tackled or a penalty occurs in their end zone, a safety worth two points is awarded to the opposing team.

20. In college football, the clock stops on first downs, while in the NFL, it stops only for incomplete passes, out-of-bounds plays, and touchdowns.

21. Beginning with a first down, the NFL passed a rule in 2023 stating that the play clock remains constant, except in the last two minutes of each half.

22. A 15-yard penalty called "roughing the passer" is issued when a defender strikes the quarterback late or too forcefully.

23. Horse-collar tackles are illegal due to their potential for injury; grabbing a player by the collar at the back of their jersey incurs a 15-yard penalty.

24. Helmet-to-helmet contact is prohibited to prevent concussions; significant violations may result in penalties and possible ejection from the game.

25. One offensive player may be in motion at the snap, but that player cannot run toward the line of scrimmage.

26. If a player contacts an opponent with the crown of their helmet, NFL targeting rules may result in a penalty.

27. The kickoff starting from the 35-yard line ncourages touchbacks, reducing the risk of concussions.

28. The 25-yard line is designated for fair catches on kickoffs, emphasizing player safety.

29. An onside kick must travel at least 10 yards before the kicking team can recover the ball.

30. Defenders must allow the punt returner to catch the ball and may signal for a fair catch to avoid contact.

31. Typically, repeated violations result in a 10-yard penalty against the offending team.

32. Intentional grounding occurs when the quarterback throws the ball without a nearby receiver, resulting in a loss of down.

33. If a defender makes contact, the play is ruled dead if a player's knee touches the ground with the ball in their possession.

34. The 'tuck rule' was eliminated in 2013, so if a quarterback loses possession of the ball while bringing it back, it's considered a fumble.

35. The attacking team incurs a five-yard penalty for a false start, defined as moving before the snap.

36. Taunting is a penalty in the NFL; officials fine players for overly aggressive behavior directed at opponents.

37. In 2015, the NFL moved the extra-point snap line to the 15-yard line for testing purposes.

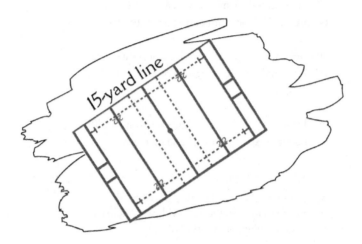

38. During field goals and extra points, defensive players must avoid being directly above the long snapper.

39. Players are required to wear jerseys with numerically allocated numbers; linemen are assigned numbers 50–79.

40. Every half ends with a "two-minute warning," allowing for strategic planning and television commercials during the break.

41. On fourth downs, teams may opt for a field goal, punt, or attempt to gain a first down, adding a strategic component to pivotal game moments.

42. The quarterback may throw the ball away outside the pocket to avoid a sack if it crosses the line of scrimmage.

3. If a penalty does not improve their situation, the offense or the defense may "decline" it.

4. On a passing play, offensive linemen who are too far downfield may prompt a penalty or ineligible receivers.

5. To avoid an illegal formation penalty, teams must have at least seven players on the line of scrimmage

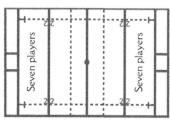

6. Players can kneel in the end zone following a punt, resulting in a touchback.

7. The play clock in high school football runs for 25 seconds, which is less than that in college and the NFL.

8. Unlike some NFL calls, defensive pass interference in college football is not reviewable or subject to investigation.

9. Considered "unnecessary roughness," excessive contact with downed players results in a 15-yard penalty.

10. The NFL adopted stricter rules on helmet-to-helmet contact in 2018, with officials determining if an ejection is warranted for targeting.

11. A ball that goes out of the end zone results in a touchback, granting possession to the defense.

52. Occasionally, offensive linemen's movements too far downfield on screen passes result in penalties for ineligible players.

53. Although rarely used, a "drop kick"—bouncing the ball before kicking it for a field goal or extra point—is still allowed.

54. The NFL permits quarterbacks and kickers to wear jersey numbers between 1 and 19.

55. Originally implemented in 2005, the "horse-collar" penalty was designed to protect players from injuries after Terrell Owens suffered a collarbone break.

56. If a team purposefully fouls during the last play, the game clock runs out, giving the other team one more chance if the outcome changes.

57. The "no-huddle offense" is often used by offensive teams to speed up play and prevent substitutions by the opposing team.

58. The NFL's "tuck rule" allowed quarterbacks to avoid turnovers by classifying slow forward motions as throws.

59. In the NFL, touchbacks on kickoffs and punts advance the ball to the 25-yard line, encouraging safer kickoff techniques.

60. Offensive players cannot move toward the line of scrimmage during the snap; they can only move laterally or backward with respect to the line.

61. A 'dead ball foul' ends the play and results in penalties applied to the next down.

62. The rules allow quarterbacks to 'spike' the ball right after the snap to stop the clock, without being penalized for intentional grounding.

63. College players expelled for targeting must remain on the sidelines for the duration of the game.

64. Teams receive three timeouts each half to stop the game, impacting strategy and clock management.

65. In college football, only one foot needs to be in bounds for a catch, while in the NFL, both feet must be in bounds for a complete catch.

66. Each NFL team receives two challenges per game; a successful challenge grants another opportunity for a challenge.

67. During the last two minutes of each half, only officials can initiate reviews; coaches are unable to challenge plays.

68. Offensive linemen are not allowed to grab or drag opponents, resulting in a 10-yard penalty for holding.

69. Football consists of four 15-minute quarters, with a halftime break, and a sudden-death overtime period in the playoffs if needed.

Chapter 6: Iconic Plays

1. Franco Harris of the Steelers caught a deflected ball in 1972 and raced into the end zone for a playoff victory against the Raiders.

2. Joe Montana's pass to Dwight Clark, known as 'The Catch,' in the NFC Championship Game propelled the 49ers to their first Super Bowl.

5. The lateral play known as 'The Music City Miracle' in the 2000 playoffs helped the Titans defeat the Bills.

6. Nick Foles of the Eagles caught a touchdown pass in Super Bowl LII, contributing to their victory over the Patriots.

3. David Tyree's "Helmet Catch" in Super Bowl XLII allowed the Giants to challenge the unbeaten Patriots.

4. Stefon Diggs scored on the game's final play in the 2018 Minneapolis Miracle, advancing the Vikings past the Saints.

7. Tony Dorsett's 99-yard touchdown in 1983 remains the longest run from scrimmage in NFL history.

8. Ken Stabler threw a last-second touchdown in "The Sea of Hands" game in 1976, helping the Raiders overcome the Dolphins.

. John Elway drove the Broncos 98 yards in ive minutes to tie the game and eventually vin in overtime in 1987.

). Dan Marino's "fake spike" against 1e Jets in 1994 tricked the entire efense and resulted in a game-vinning touchdown.

11. Roger Staubach popularized "The Hail Mary" in 1975 with a last-second touchdown throw for the Cowboys to defeat the Vikings.

12. Devin Hester returned the opening kickoff for a touchdown in Super Bowl XLI in 2006.

3. Lynn Swann showcased the elegance of the receiver position and won MVP honors for his spectacular Super Bowl X performances.

4. Antonio Freeman's 2000 "He did WHAT?!" reception for the Packers was a remarkable, bobbling touchdown catch n overtime.

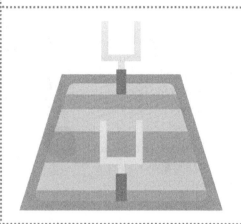

5. In 1978, the Raiders fumbled into the end zone for a controversial score against the Chargers, known as the "Holy Roller."

6. Ben Roethlisberger's crucial tackle saved the Steelers after Jerome Bettis's fumble in the 2005 AFC Divisional Round.

17. Kellen Winslow Sr. caught 13 passes despite injuries during the 1982 "Epic in Miami," helping the Chargers defeat the Dolphins.

18. Desmond Howard earned MVP honors for the Packers with his 99-yard kickoff return in Super Bowl XXXI.

9. In 2012, Jets quarterback Mark Sanchez ran into the backside of his lineman, resulting in a Patriots score during the infamous "Butt Fumble."

20. One of the most well-known pick-sixes in NFL history was Willie Brown's 75-yard interception return in Super Bowl XI.

21. In -13°F conditions, Bart Starr slipped into the end zone to secure the 1967 NFL Championship for the Packers.

22. Herman Edwards of the Eagles recovered a fumble and scored to defeat the Giants in the "Miracle at the Meadowlands" in 1978.

23. Randy Moss's "Three catches, three touchdowns" performance on Thanksgiving Day stunned the Cowboys.

24. Tony Hill caught a deflected Hail Mary pass to defeat the Vikings in a playoff game for the Cowboys in 1977.

25. James Harrison's 100-yard interception return in Super Bowl XLIII is still the longest defensive play in Super Bowl history.

26. Cody Parkey of the Bears missed a field goal, ending their playoff hopes in 2018.

27. Reggie White's multiple sacks during Super Bowl XXXI helped the Packers defeat the Patriots.

28. Marshawn Lynch's 67-yard "Beast Quake" run in 2011 broke nine tackles and caused seismic activity in Seattle.

29. After his father's passing, Brett Favre's "Monday Night Miracle" featured four touchdown passes in the first half against the Raiders.

30. Troy Polamalu's one-handed interception against the Titans showcased his agility and awareness in 2009.

31. Ray Rice's fourth-and-29 conversion helped the Ravens secure a postseason victory over the Chargers in 2012.

32. Terrell Owens' 1998 postseason "The Catch II" guaranteed a last-second victory for the 49ers over the Packers.

33. Santonio Holmes' toe-tap catch in Super Bowl XLIII helped the Steelers defeat the Cardinals in the final moments.

34. Jim Marshall infamously returned a fumble the wrong way for a safety during his "Wrong Way Run" in 1964.

35. Mike Jones tackled Kevin Dyson just one yard short, sealing the Rams' victory in Super Bowl XXXIV.

36. Marcus Allen's 74-yard touchdown run in Super Bowl XVIII secured the Raiders' victory over Washington.

37. Alex Smith's last-minute heroics in the 49ers' "Greatest Game Ever Played" comeback against the Saints were remarkable.

38. Julian Edelman's juggling catch in Super Bowl LI was pivotal in the Patriots' 28-3 comeback over the Falcons.

39. In the 2012 playoffs, Vernon Davis caught a last-second touchdown for the 49ers against the Saints.

40. Billy "White Shoes" Johnson's 1978 "Hail Mary" delivered the Oilers an exciting last-second playoff victory over the Bengals.

41. The term 'Hail Mary' originated from Roger Staubach's 1975 game-winning touchdown pass for the Cowboys.

42. Adam Vinatieri kicked a game-winning field goal for the Patriots in heavy snow during 'The Snow Bowl' in 2001.

43. Frank Reich led the Bills to a 32-point comeback against the Oilers in the 1993 playoffs, the largest in NFL history.

44. Michael Vick's 46-yard touchdown run against the Vikings in 2002 showcased his explosive speed.

45. Jerome Simpson scored a gravity-defying front-flip touchdown for the Bengals.

46. The Bears defeated the Eagles in near-zero visibility conditions during the "Fog Bowl" in 1989.

47. Steve Young's zigzagging 49-yard touchdown run against the Vikings in 1988 became an all-time classic.

48. Larry Fitzgerald's 64-yard touchdown in Super Bowl XLIII temporarily gave the Cardinals the lead late in the game.

49. Joe Flacco's 70-yard touchdown pass to Jacoby Jones was decisive in the 2013 playoffs against the Broncos.

50. Odell Beckham Jr.'s one-handed catch against the Cowboys in 2014 became an instant classic.

51. Bo Jackson showcased his incredible speed and power with a 91-yard touchdown run on Monday Night Football in 1987.

52. The Saints executed a surprise onside kick to start the second half in Super Bowl XLIV, a pivotal play in their 2009 championship win.

53. Jerry Rice's 215-yard receiving game in Super Bowl XXIII remains unsurpassed.

Super Bowl

54. In 2015, Cam Newton's "Superman" leap across the Packers' defense became a legendary moment in his MVP season.

55. Eric Dickerson's 1987 "Chase-Down" by Darrell Green highlighted his unmatched speed.

56. Brian Urlacher's pursuit of Michael Vick defined his career in 2000.

57. Kurt Warner's performance in Super Bowl XXXIV, which included 414 passing yards, helped the Rams secure victory.

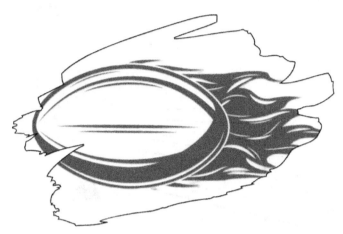

58. Jim Brown's five-touchdown game in 1959 remains one of the top performances by a running back.

59. Peyton Manning's record-breaking 55 touchdown passes in 2013 concluded with a stunning TD to Demaryius Thomas.

60. Ken Anderson's 447-yard, five-touchdown performance helped the Bengals defeat the Oilers in 1975.

61. Tom Brady's last-minute 91-yard drive against the Saints in 2013 was a thrilling climax to the game.

62. The 2001 "Kickoff Return Gone Wrong" saw the Colts tackle the incorrect returner, leading to a mishap.

63. Odell Beckham Jr.'s '3-Finger' catch in pregame warm-ups in 2015 drew comparisons to Spider-Man.

64. Eli Manning's turn and escape to throw a miraculous pass to David Tyree remains one of the top moments in Super Bowl history.

65. Tim Tebow's 80-yard overtime pass to Demaryius Thomas secured a playoff victory against the Steelers in 2011.

66. Barry Sanders' 220-yard performance in 1997 showcased his incredible speed and agility.

67. Aaron Rodgers' 60-yard Hail Mary against the Lions in 2016 resulted in a game-winning touchdown.

68. Jerry Rice's 92-yard touchdown in his rookie season demonstrated his lasting influence on the game.

69. The 'Immaculate Reception,' a famous deflected catch by Franco Harris from a Terry Bradshaw pass, occurred in the 1972 playoffs.

70. Devin Hester's 108-yard kickoff return for a touchdown remains a prominent NFL record.

Chapter 7: The Super Bowl

1. William Perry, a defensive lineman, scored an incredible running touchdown in Super Bowl XX.

2. "Mean Joe" Greene's Coca-Cola commercial aired during the 1979 Super Bowl before Super Bowl XX.

3. Eleven million pounds of potato chips are expected to be eaten on Super Bowl Sunday.

4. Super Bowl tickets in the 1980s sometimes cost less than $100; today, the least expensive seats can cost around $5,000.

5. Eli Manning won two Super Bowls with the Giants, defeating the Patriots on both occasions.

6. Every Super Bowl participant receives a bonus check, with winning team players receiving more than losing team players.

7. Super Bowl LIII had the lowest score in Super Bowl history, with a total of 16 points, while Super Bowl XLVII experienced a 34-minute power outage, earning it the nickname 'The Blackout Bowl.'

8. The Buffalo Bills set a Super Bowl record with nine turnovers in Super Bowl XXVII.

9. Stiffer broadcast rules emerged following the wardrobe malfunction during Janet Jackson and Justin Timberlake's halftime show in 2004.

10. Before Super Bowl III, Joe Namath famously promised a victory for the underdog Jets, who went on to defeat the Colts.

11. John Elway secured his first Super Bowl victory in Super Bowl XXXII after four attempts, winning with the Denver Broncos.

12. Lady Gaga surprised the audience and social media with a jump from the roof during her halftime performance at Super Bowl LI.

13. Super Bowl Sunday sees the consumption of over 1.4 billion chicken wings across the United States.

14. The Super Bowl is one of the most-watched sporting events worldwide, broadcast in nearly 200 countries.

15. No NFL teams have ever shut each other out in a Super Bowl.

16. The Tampa Bay Buccaneers became the first team to compete in a Super Bowl at their home stadium during Super Bowl LV.

17. On Super Bowl Sunday, approximately 30 million pounds of appetizers, including chips and dips, are consumed.

18. Peyton Manning is the only quarterback to win two Super Bowls with different teams (the Colts and the Broncos).

19. Phil Simms was the first player to exclaim, 'I'm going to Disney World!' after being named MVP of the 1987 Super Bowl.

20. Prince's performance during Super Bowl XLI in 2007 is often regarded as the best halftime show in the rain.

21. Super Bowl commercials have become as famous as the game itself, often featuring well-known and expensive campaigns.

22. Super Bowl I was not a sellout; tickets were sold until game day.

23. Originally called the "AFL-NFL World Championship Game," Super Bowl I took place in 1967.

24. Super Bowl LIV marked the first time two teams with red as their primary color (the 49ers and the Chiefs) competed in the Super Bowl, with the Chiefs wearing red and the 49ers wearing white.

25. The Tampa Bay Buccaneers won Super Bowl LV, becoming the first team in their home city to win a Super Bowl.

26. Super Bowl LVI had an average ticket price of almost $10,000, making it the most expensive Super Bowl to date.

7. Jalen Hurts and Patrick Mahomes made history in Super Bowl LVII in 2023 as the first matchup of two Black starting quarterbacks.

8. Super Bowl rings, featuring the team's emblem, can be worth up to $5 million each.

1. Tickets for the inaugural Super Bowl in 1967 originally cost just $12.

2. The New Orleans Saints executed a surprise onside kick at the start of the second half in Super Bowl XLIV, which played a crucial role in their victory over the Indianapolis Colts.

3. Terry Bradshaw and Joe Montana were the first quarterbacks to achieve four Super Bowl victories.

4. The tradition of the 'Gatorade shower,' where players pour Gatorade on the winning coach, began with the New York Giants in the 1980s.

7. Rihanna performed at the halftime show of the 2023 Super Bowl, marking her first live performance in over five years.

8. The San Francisco 49ers achieved the largest margin of victory in Super Bowl history, winning 55-10 against the Denver Broncos in Super Bowl XXIV.

29. Super Bowl Sunday is one of the busiest days for pizza delivery, with demand surging during the game.

30. Super Bowl Sunday is the second largest food consumption day in the United States, following Thanksgiving.

Super Bowl Sunday

35. The Monday following the Super Bowl is one of the most commonly taken sick days by employees.

36. Vince Lombardi, the legendary coach of the Green Bay Packers, led his team to victory in the first two Super Bowls, inspiring the naming of the "Lombardi Trophy."

39. The lengthy halftime performance contributes to the average Super Bowl game length of approximately three hours and forty-four minutes.

40. The Chicago Bears' 46-10 victory over the New England Patriots in Super Bowl XX remains one of the most lopsided games in Super Bowl history.

41. A 30-second commercial during the Super Bowl is expected to cost more than $7 million in 2024.

42. The Dallas Cowboys and Pittsburgh Steelers have each played in eight Super Bowls, the most of any franchise.

43. The Green Bay Packers won the first two Super Bowls under legendary coach Vince Lombardi.

45. In Super Bowl LIII, Rams punter Johnny Hekker executed a 65-yard punt, the longest in Super Bowl history.

44. It was not until the early 1990s that well-known performers began to take the stage at the Super Bowl halftime show, which had previously featured college marching bands.

46. Willie Parker of the Pittsburgh Steelers made the longest touchdown run in Super Bowl history, covering 75 yards in Super Bowl XL.

47. The Los Angeles Rams became the first team to win a Super Bowl in their home city, triumphing at SoFi Stadium during Super Bowl LVI.

48. In Super Bowl XXIX, the San Francisco 49ers and San Diego Chargers combined for a total of 75 points, the highest in Super Bowl history.

49. The New England Patriots hold the record for the most Super Bowl appearances, having played in the big game eleven times.

60. The New York Jets' victory in Super Bowl III inspired the AFL-NFL merger, as they were the first AFL team to win the Super Bowl.

51. For Super Bowl I, the NFL reimbursed each player's travel expenses with a $15 check.

52. Each NFL team participating in the Super Bowl receives 108 footballs, divided into 54 for game use and 54 for practice.

53. Roman numerals are used to designate Super Bowls to avoid confusion since the title reflects the season rather than the year in which the game is played.

Super bowl

$15

54. The Pittsburgh Steelers and the New England Patriots are tied for the most Super Bowl titles in NFL history, each with six championships.

55. The San Francisco 49ers scored the highest total points in a Super Bowl, with 55 points against the Denver Broncos in Super Bowl XXIV.

56. The 'High Five' craze, attributed to Dodgers players Dusty Baker and Glenn Burke in 1977, became a significant part of NFL culture, especially during Super Bowl events.

57. The Super Bowl coin toss has resulted in tails 30 times, slightly more often than heads.

58. Each year, the Super Bowl generates nearly $14 billion in economic activity across the nation.

59. Since Super Bowl LI, the only Super Bowl to go into overtime, no other Super Bowl has gone into extra time.

60. Typically attracting around 100 million viewers, the Super Bowl is the most-watched television event in the United States each year.

61. The Pete Rozelle Trophy, named after the former NFL Commissioner, is awarded to the Super Bowl MVP.

62. The production cost of the Vince Lombardi Trophy is approximately $50,000.

63. Designed by Tiffany & Co., the 7-pound Vince Lombardi Trophy is awarded to the Super Bowl champion, and the winning team receives it on the field immediately after the game.

64. Joe Namath became the first player to win the Super Bowl MVP for guaranteeing and then delivering a victory in Super Bowl III.

65. Tom Brady holds the record for the most Super Bowl victories, with seven championships.

66. At age 43, Tom Brady became the oldest quarterback to start in a Super Bowl during Super Bowl LV.

Chapter 8: Famous Players and Records

1. Barry Sanders ran for over 1,000 yards in each of his ten NFL seasons —an achievement matched by few players.

2. Brett Favre was the first quarterback to complete 500 career touchdown passes.

6. Derrick Henry set a career-high with 247 rushing yards against the Seattle Seahawks in 2021.

3. Chris Johnson recorded the fastest 40-yard dash time at the NFL Combine in 2008, finishing in 4.24 seconds.

7. Jerry Rice holds the record for the most career receiving yards with 22,895 yards, more than any other player.

8. Jim Brown holds the record for the highest career average rushing yards per game at 104.3.

4. Dan Marino set the single-season passing record with 5,084 yards in 1984, which stood for many years.

9. Joe Montana is the only quarterback to win four Super Bowls without losing one.

5. Only one player, Deion Sanders, has scored a touchdown in both the Super Bowl and the World Series.

10. Johnny Unitas was the first quarterback to surpass 40,000 career passing yards.

11. Lawrence Taylor is the only defensive player to have won the NFL MVP award.

12. Peyton Manning holds the record for the most touchdown passes in a single season, with 55, while playing for the Denver Broncos.

3. Randy Moss recorded 1,200 receiving yards in his rookie year (1998), marking one of the best starts for a wide receiver.

4. Randy Moss set a single-game touchdown record with four touchdowns against the Chicago Bears in 2007.

7. The New Orleans Saints scored the fastest touchdown in NFL history just twelve seconds into a game in 2019.

8. Chuck Howley was the first defensive player to win the Super Bowl MVP, achieving this feat in Super Bowl V.

Super Bowl MVP

15. Terrell Owens ranks third in career receiving yards with 15,934 but was not inducted into the Hall of Fame until several years after his eligibility.

16. Tyreek Hill reached a maximum speed of 23.24 mph in a game, making him one of the fastest players in NFL history according to GPS data.

19. Joe Namath is noted for leading the New York Jets to their first Super Bowl victory in Super Bowl III, but he did not score the first touchdown; it was a running play.

20. The Oakland Raiders were the first wild card team to win the Super Bowl, achieving this in Super Bowl XV.

21. Jim Brown ranks among the best running backs, with a minimum of 1,000 carries and an average of 5.2 yards per carry.

22. Patrick Mahomes recorded the highest passer rating for a single season, achieving a rating of 118.8 in 2018.

23. Norm Van Brocklin holds the record for the most passing yards in a single game, throwing for 554 yards in 1951.

554 yards

24. Justin Tucker set the record for the longest field goal in NFL history with a 66-yard kick for the Baltimore Ravens.

25. Ed Reed set the NFL record for the longest interception return with a 107-yard return in 2008, breaking his own 106-yard record from 2004.

26. The 99-yard touchdown run has been accomplished multiple times, with the Miami Dolphins having the most recent one. The longest run from scrimmage in NFL history is 99 yards.

27. Jerry Rice holds the record for the most career-receiving touchdowns with 197.

28. Jerry Rice accumulated over 2,245 receiving yards during his playoff career.

29. Michael Strahan recorded the fifth most career sacks by a player in NFL history, finishing with 141.5.

NFL 141.5 history

30. Jim Hardy and George Blanda are among the players who share the record for the most interceptions thrown in a single game, with eight.

31. LaDainian Tomlinson set the record for the most rushing touchdowns in a single season with 31 during the 2006 NFL season.

32. The San Francisco 49ers scored eight touchdowns in Super Bowl XXIV, the most in a single Super Bowl game.

33. Gale Sayers and Dub Jones share the NFL record for the most touchdowns scored in a single game, with six.

34. In 1960, Johnny Unitas became the first NFL player to secure a million-dollar contract.

35. Doug Williams was the first African American quarterback to win a Super Bowl, leading the Washington Redskins to victory in Super Bowl XXII.

36. At Super Bowl LV in 2021, Sarah Thomas made history as the first female official to officiate a Super Bowl.

42. George Blanda holds the record for the most career interceptions thrown, with 276.

43. Ben Roethlisberger ranks among the highest in NFL history for passing yards in a single game, completing 582 yards in 2014.

44. Jerry Rice holds the record for the most career receptions in NFL history, with 1,549 catches.

37. O.J. Simpson became the first NFL player to rush for 2,000 yards in a single season in 1973.

38. Brett Favre won back-to-back NFL MVP awards three times, dominating the league from 1995 to 1997.

39. Joe Namath is the only player to have won the NFL MVP award, Super Bowl MVP, and the Heisman Trophy.

40. Deion Sanders is known for his punt return touchdowns, ranking among the leaders in NFL history.

41. As of 2021, the record for the longest touchdown pass in NFL history is 99 yards, a feat that has occurred multiple times.

45. Emmitt Smith holds the record for the most rushing touchdowns in NFL history, with 164.

46. Ray Lewis is one of the most prolific tacklers in NFL history, finishing his career with nearly 2,000 tackles.

47. Morten Andersen played in 382 games over 25 seasons, holding the record for the most games played in NFL history.

48. Drew Brees holds the record for the most consecutive games with a touchdown pass, achieving 54.

49. Charles Haley holds the record for the most fumble recoveries in a single season, achieving this feat twice.

50. George Blanda set the record for the most interceptions thrown in a single season with 42 in 1962.

51. Tom Dempsey scored the most points by a kicker in a single game, with 16 points in 1970.

52. Cooper Kupp recorded the highest single-season total with 145 receptions in 2021.

53. Eric Dickerson holds the record for the most rushing yards in a single playoff game, with 248 yards.

54. Franco Harris rushed for 158 yards in Super Bowl IX, making him the player with the most rushing yards in a single Super Bowl game.

55. In 2021, Tom Brady became the first quarterback to reach 600 career touchdown passes.

56. Tom Brady has won the Super Bowl MVP award five times, more than any other player in NFL history.

57. Walter Payton held the record for the most career rushing yards at 16,726 until Emmitt Smith surpassed it in 2002.

Chapter 9: Stadiums

1. Lambeau Field (Green Bay Packers) is the first NFL stadium continually in constant use, opening in 1957.

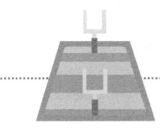

4. With about 76,000 capacity, Arrowhead Stadium (Kansas City Chiefs) is among the largest outdoor venues.

5. The New York Giants called Yankee Stadium home prior to the construction of Giants Stadium in 1976.

6. After Hurricane Katrina and the damage to the Superdome in New Orleans, the Saints returned in 2006 to host the "Homecoming."

7. Giants Stadium in New Jersey maintained the most continuous sell-through record from 1976 until its closure in 2010.

2. Soldier Field (Chicago Bears), originally built in 1924, is the oldest NFL stadium ever based on age.

3. The Los Angeles Memorial Coliseum has hosted the Rams, Raiders, and Trojans at different intervals, apart from two Olympic Games (1932 and 1984).

8. Originally the largest NFL stadium, FedEx Field (Washington Commanders) had a capacity of about 90,000 in the early 2000s.

9. Ford Field (Detroit Lions) retains Detroit's industrial heritage, situated inside an abandoned structure.

10. Unlike a dome, U.S. Bank Stadium (Minnesota Vikings) boasts a translucent roof that allows guests to feel connected to the outside.

11. AT&T Stadium (Dallas Cowboys) boasts one of the largest high-definition TV displays in the world, spanning sixty yards across the field.

12. Allegiant Stadium (Las Vegas Raiders) features a large torch honoring the late club owner Al Davis.

3. The retractable roof of Mercedes-Benz Stadium appears to the Atlanta Falcons like a camera lens.

4. SoFi Stadium (Los Angeles) is the most expensive NFL facility, costing around $5 billion.

15. Among the loudest NFL arenas, Lumen Field (Seattle Seahawks) is designed to amplify crowd noise.

16. The field at State Farm Stadium (Arizona Cardinals) can roll in and out due to its fully retractable design.

7. Lucas Oil Stadium (Indianapolis Colts) has a 120-yard-long window view of the city skyline thanks to its unique movable roof.

8. Highmark Stadium (Buffalo Bills) is one of the few outdoor venues in a cold city without a dome or retractable roof.

9. Mile High Stadium (Denver Broncos) ranks highest among NFL facilities at 5,280 feet above sea level.

20. Levi's Stadium (San Francisco 49ers) features a green roof designed for optimal environmental efficiency in cooling.

21. Arrowhead Stadium holds a Guinness World Record for the loudest stadium crowd noise at 142.2 decibels.

World Record

22. AT&T Stadium can accommodate the largest NFL capacity-about 100,000 people-using standing-room tickets.

23. The Rose Bowl has the highest NFL attendance ever, with 103,525 people for a Rams game in 1957.

24. Ford Field recorded the lowest Super Bowl temperature ever at 2¬∞F outside.

5. The Superdome has hosted the most Super Bowls, with seven games.

6. MetLife Stadium (Giants/Jets) was the first outdoor stadium to host a Super Bowl in cold weather.

7. Following a 2013 power outage, Caesars Superdome held the longest Super Bowl game by time.

28. Lumen Field has the highest incidence of false starts due to crowd noise.

29. Bank of America Stadium (Carolina Panthers) implemented fully online ticketing starting in 2015.

30. Oakland Coliseum was the last combined NFL/MLB facility until the Raiders left in 2020.

31. Comprising over 2,000 glass panels, U.S. Bank Stadium allows natural light to flood the venue.

32. Mercedes-Benz Stadium in Atlanta offers the lowest concession prices among NFL venues.

33. Gillette Stadium features a lighthouse that commemorates New England's maritime heritage.

34. Known for its long-standing tailgating traditions, Arrowhead Stadium is particularly famous for its BBQ.

35. Visitors to Nissan Stadium (Tennessee Titans) can walk from downtown Nashville via a nearby pedestrian bridge.

36. Fans at Lambeau Field can "leap" into the stands, a unique touchdown celebration.

37. Tickets for standing-room allow fans to view concourses at AT&T Stadium.

38. Levi's Stadium provides guests with free solar-powered phone charging stations.

FREE

Solar-powered phone charging stations.

39. M&T Bank Stadium (Baltimore Ravens) is the first NFL stadium to earn LEED Gold certification for environmental sustainability.

40. TIAA Bank Field (Jacksonville Jaguars) features a pool cabana where fans can swim during the game.

43. Gillette Stadium is surrounded by a large complex that includes stores, restaurants, and entertainment options.

44. There is a full-scale pirate ship at Raymond James Stadium (Tampa Bay Buccaneers).

47. MetLife Stadium serves as the home field for both the Giants and the Jets.

48. The Caesars Superdome is known for its unique circular architecture.

49. Lumen Field is unique to Seattle, located near the famous Pike Place Market.

50. SoFi Stadium features a 4K double-sided video board suspended above the field.

51. Mercedes-Benz Stadium was the first NFL venue to adopt fully cashless payments.

41. Empower Field at Mile High offers stunning views of the Rocky Mountains.

42. Allegiant Stadium honors U.S. military members and is one of the few facilities to do so, given its proximity to the Las Vegas Strip.

45. Nissan Stadium offers beautiful views adjacent to the Cumberland River.

46. Heinz Field (Pittsburgh Steelers) is notable for its unique location at the confluence of three rivers.

52. State Farm Stadium is equipped with modern heating and cooling systems for the field.

53. Hard Rock Stadium features a roof that provides solar illumination for the playing field.

54. Allegiant Stadium is designed for 5G connectivity, enhancing fan engagement.

5G connectivity

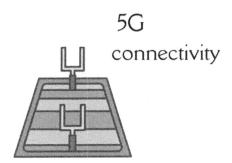

55. Levi's Stadium provides guests with quick replays through a dedicated smartphone app.

56. Ford Field features the largest LED screen in the league, measuring 65,000 square feet.

57. The design of Lucas Oil Stadium incorporates acoustics to enhance audience experience and capacity.

58. AT&T Stadium features one of the largest high-definition screens in the world.

59. Lambeau Field features a guest interactive Hall of Fame exhibit.

60. The "Dawg Pound," known for its passionate fans, was originally located at Energy Stadium (Cleveland Browns).

61. The Kansas City Chiefs are known for their "Chiefs Kingdom" network, which unites supporters across the Midwest.

62. Lambeau Field is often referred to as "The Frozen Tundra," especially noted for its cold weather games.

63. Allegiant Stadium showcases Las Vegas with neon lights and themed zones throughout the venue.

64. FedEx Field has implemented a sensory section designed for NFL viewers with autism.

65. Gillette Stadium commemorates New England's maritime history with its lighthouse feature.

66. U.S. Bank Stadium incorporates design elements inspired by Minnesota's Nordic heritage.

67. AT&T Stadium features an extensive art collection, making it as much a museum as a stadium.

68. Highmark Stadium's open-air design reflects Buffalo's working-class ethos.

69. Levi's Stadium promotes sustainability through solar panels and recycled water systems.

Chapter 10: NFL Teams

The Arizona Cardinals, the first professional football team in the U.S., were founded in 1898.

2. Originally based in Chicago, the Arizona Cardinals have a rich heritage, and they moved to St. Louis before finally settling in Arizona.

3. The Atlanta Falcons made their first Super Bowl appearance in 1998, losing to the Denver Bro.

4. Founded in 1965, the Atlanta Falcons are the only team in their division that has never won a Super Bowl.

5. The Atlanta Falcons were the first NFL team to use a "cleaning" robot to maintain stadium operations during games.

6. Established in 1996, the Baltimore Ravens are the only NFL team named after a literary character, Edgar Allan Poe's "The Raven."

7. The Baltimore Ravens won their first Super Bowl in 2000, just four years after their establishment.

8. The Buffalo Bills appeared in four consecutive Super Bowls from 1990 to 1993, losing each time.

9. The passionate Buffalo Bills fan base, often referred to as "Bills Mafia," has gained national attention for their tailgating and support.

10. The Buffalo Bills, founded in 1960, were named after the famous showman Buffalo Bill Cody.

11. The Chicago Bears are known for their legendary defenses, particularly during their Super Bowl XX-winning season in 1985.

12. The Chicago Bears, originally known as the Decatur Staleys, are one of the oldest franchises in the league, established in 1919.

13. The Chicago Bears were among the first champions in league history, winning the NFL Championship in 1921.

14. Although they have not won a Super Bowl, the Cincinnati Bengals reached the championship game in 1981 and again in 2022.

Championship
1981
↓
2022

15. Paul Brown was the the inaugural head coach of the Cincinnati Bengals, starting in 1968.

16. The Cleveland Browns' tumultuous history has been shaped by several ownership changes and significant games, including the "Drive" and the "Fumble."

17. Founded in 1946, the Cleveland Browns were co-founded by Paul Brown, who also served as their first head coach.

18. The Dallas Cowboys, who gained popularity in the late 1970s, are often referred to as "America's Team."

19. With five Super Bowl championships, the Dallas Cowboys are one of the most successful teams in NFL history.

20. The Denver Broncos have had several Hall of Fame quarterbacks, including Peyton Manning and John Elway.

21. The Detroit Lions, one of the oldest franchises in the league, were originally part of the American Football League (AFL) but have struggled to win championships.

22. Founded in 1930, the Detroit Lions have not won a championship since 1957.

23. With over 538,000 owners, the Green Bay Packers are the only community-owned team in the NFL.

24. The Green Bay Packers won both of the first two Super Bowls, Super Bowl I in 1967 and Super Bowl II in 1968.

25. Founded in 2002 as an expansion team, the Houston Texans are the most recent franchise added to the NFL.

26. When the Houston Oilers left, the NFL granted the Houston Texans the 32nd franchise.

27. The Indianapolis Colts, originally the Baltimore Colts, relocated on March 28, 1984.

28. The Jacksonville Jaguars are one of the younger teams in the league, granted expansion rights in 1993.

29. The Kansas City Chiefs won their first Super Bowl in 1970 and their second in 2020, marking a 50-year gap between championships.

30. Originally known as the Dallas Texans, the team moved to Kansas City in 1963 and became the Kansas City Chiefs.

31. The Los Angeles Chargers were originally based in Los Angeles before relocating to San Diego in 1961 and were one of the first AFL teams.

32. The Los Angeles Rams, extremely popular in Southern California, have the highest average attendance in the NFL.

33. The Los Angeles Rams returned to Los Angeles in 2016 after spending over twenty years in St. Louis.

34. The Los Angeles Rams were the first NFL team to feature their logo on their helmets, debuting it in 1948.

35. The Miami Dolphins became the first team in NFL history to win a Super Bowl following an undefeated regular season.

36. The Minnesota Vikings are celebrated for their "Purple People Eaters," a dominant defensive line from the late 1960s and early 1970s.

37. The Minnesota Vikings, despite never winning a Super Bowl, have appeared in four championship games, the most without a victory.

38. The Minnesota Vikings introduced "Viktor the Viking" in 1978, becoming the first NFL team to have a mascot.

39. The New England Patriots are the only team to have started a season with a losing record and then won the Super Bowl.

40. The New England Patriots won three Super Bowl championships in four years-2001, 2003, and 2004-leading the 2000s with their success.

41. The New England Patriots hold the best winning percentage in NFL postseason history.

Winning percentage 100%

42. The New England Patriots were originally known as the Boston Patriots when they were founded in 1960, changing their name in 1971.

43. After suffering in the aftermath of Hurricane Katrina, the New Orleans Saints triumphed in Super Bowl XLIV, winning their first championship in 2010.

44. Established in 1967, the New Orleans Saints' name is derived from the jazz music associated with the city.

45. The rivalry between the Chicago Bears and New York Giants, which dates back to 1926, is the most frequently contested matchup in NFL history.

46. The New York Giants and New York Jets share MetLife Stadium, making them one of the unique pairings of teams sharing a home venue.

47. The Washington Commanders and New York Giants have a long-standing rivalry, making them one of the NFL's oldest rivalries.

48. The New York Giants won their first NFL title in 1927, claiming the league championship.

49. The New York Jets made history by defeating the Baltimore Colts in Super Bowl III, claiming their first championship.

50. The Jets were originally known as the New York Titans before changing their name in 1963.

51. he Oakland Raiders, established in 1960, have had a tumultuous history, including relocations to Los Angeles, back to Oakland, and finally to Las Vegas.

52. The Philadelphia Eagles were founded in 1933 when a group of businessmen sought to establish a team in Philadelphia by acquiring the rights to an NFL franchise.

53. The Philadelphia Eagles won their first Super Bowl championship in 2018 by defeating the New England Patriots in Super Bowl LII.

54. The Pittsburgh Steelers have won six Super Bowl championships, the most in NFL history.

55. Founded in 1933, the Pittsburgh Steelers are the oldest team in the AFC.

56. The San Diego Chargers, established in 1960, were the first team to sign a quarterback to a $1 million contract.

57. The San Francisco 49ers have appeared in eight Super Bowls, winning their first five from 1981 to 1994.

58. The quarterback-receiver duo of Jerry Rice and Joe Montana is considered one of the most successful in NFL history.

59. Established in 1946 as part of the All-America Football Conference (AAFC), the San Francisco 49ers later joined the NFL.

60. The Seattle Seahawks began their NFL journey in 1976 as members of the AFC and switched to the NFC in 2002.

61. After missing the Super Bowl in 2005, the Seattle Seahawks made their second appearance in 2014.

62. The Seattle Seahawks defeated the Denver Broncos in a memorable Super Bowl held in 2014.

63. The Tampa Bay Buccaneers became the first team to win a Super Bowl at their home stadium when they won Super Bowl LV.

64. The Tampa Bay Buccaneers have experimented with various team colors and logos over the years, reflecting their evolving identity.

65. The Tennessee Titans made their Super Bowl debut in the 1999 season, losing Super Bowl XXXIV to the St. Louis Rams.

66. The Tennessee Titans, originally the Houston Oilers, were established in 1960 and relocated to Nashville in 1997.

67. The Washington Commanders, originally known as the Boston Braves, have undergone several name changes throughout history.

Chapter 11: Equipment Evolution

1. Early footballs were originally round, resembling a soccer ball more than modern footballs, and were made of pigskin

2. Late 19th-century athletes often wore minimal padding, typically just leather helmets, to prevent injuries.

3. Helmets were first used in football in 1893, originally intended to prevent head injuries.

7. Intended to improve aerodynamics and throwing accuracy, the NFL introduced the "spiral" ball in 1960.

4. Face masks, designed to protect players' faces and prevent injuries, were first introduced in the late 1940s.

8. Modern football helmets, designed with polycarbonate and foam for impact cushioning to reduce concussions, became popular in the 1970s. Mouthguards also gained popularity for protecting players' teeth and jaws.

5. In the early 20th century, footballs became more elongated, a design improvement that made throwing easier.

9. The first synthetic grass revolutionized the playing field when it was introduced at Houston's Astrodome in 1965.

6. The first set of football shoulder pads, designed in the 1930s, enhanced protection against impacts for players.

10. Introduced in the 1980s, padded gloves were designed to enhance grip and provide hand protection.

11. The "Pro Shield" helmet, designed in the 1980s, provides athletes with improved comfort and airflow.

2. The 1990s saw the integration of lightweight and flexible materials into shoulder pad esign, significantly enhancing mobility.

3. In 2011, the NFL implemented consistent helmet testing to enhance player safety and erformance.

4. In 2015, the NFL introduced the "concussion spotter" rule, requiring an independent bserver to assess athletes for potential head injuries.

. Customized footwear has evolved, lowing players to select cleats tailored specific playing conditions and ositions.

16. "Smart" helmets, which measure force and monitor head impacts, began to appear in the 2010s.

17. Modern NFL team jerseys now feature high-tech moisture-wicking fabrics designed to keep players cool and dry.

. In the 2010s, some teams xperimented with digital wristbands or field communication and play-lling.

20. The NFL employs a "Game Day" equipment manager to ensure that each team's equipment complies with league standards.

In 2014, the NFL introduced a new me ball equipped with an ectronic chip to track ball movement d enhance officiating accuracy.

21. Players now have access to various training gear, including agility ladders and resistance bands, to enhance performance.

2. Technologies for instant replays d video reviews have revolutionized am strategy and prepared equipment or games.

24. The kicking tee, which elevates the ball for greater kicking accuracy, has been a standard in the NFL since the 1970s.

. Many teams now utilize 3D printing chnology to create custom outhguards and protective gear for hletes.

25. The invention of sports bras in the 1990s provided female athletes with greater comfort and support during competitions.

26. In the 2000s, padded compression shirts gained popularity for providing athletes with additional protection while maintaining flexibility.

27. The NFL has witnessed the emergence of advanced medical technologies, such as portable ultrasound devices, for assessing injuries on the sidelines.

28. Coaches today utilize tablet technology on the sidelines to review plays and provide real-time feedback to players.

29. Emerging in the 1990s, "injury reports" have contributed to more standardized approaches regarding equipment related to player health.

30. Customized ankle braces provide specific support for certain athletes without compromising on-field flexibility.

31. Materials research has led to the development of stronger, lighter footballs that better withstand weather conditions.

32. The NFL mandates that all game balls be inflated to a specific pressure, promoting uniformity in handling and performance.

33. Goalposts have evolved from basic wooden structures to modern high-strength steel poles engineered to withstand extreme weather.

34. Gloves equipped with grip-enhancing technology are now common, allowing receivers to catch throws under challenging conditions.

35. Hydration systems have evolved from basic water bottles into advanced stations that monitor players' fluid intake during games.

36. The use of impact-absorbing materials in helmets has improved their effectiveness in reducing head injuries.

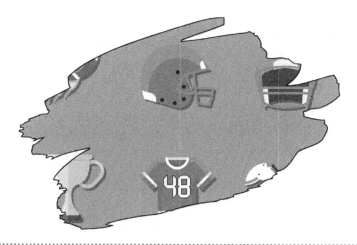

37. In 2020, the NFL began utilizing "virtual reality" technology to help players practice scenarios and enhance their decision-making skills.

38. Kickers now use specialized kicking shoes designed for optimal contact with the football.

39. On the field, lightweight football equipment has enhanced athletes' speed and agility, thereby improving their performance.

40. Players can customize their equipment with unique designs or tailored fits for enhanced performance and comfort.

41. Several teams provide players with recovery tools, including cold baths and percussion massagers, as part of their equipment package.

42. The incidence of concussions in helmets has significantly decreased due to the use of foam and other modern materials.

43. Wind-resistant footballs have improved passing accuracy in cold-weather games.

44. In 2021, the NFL announced a new helmet design primarily aimed at reducing concussions and enhancing player safety.

45. The NFL has implemented strict rules prohibiting the use of performance-enhancing drugs, which have influenced equipment and training strategies.

46. Today, the game heavily relies on goal-line technology to ensure accurate calls on critical plays.

47. To enhance safety, the NFL introduced rules requiring players to wear knee and thigh protectors in 2013.

48. Tracking technology and "next-generation" statistics have influenced equipment design and performance assessment methods.

49. Modern training facilities incorporate specialized technologies, such as virtual reality headsets, to simulate game scenarios for training.

50. Training methods have evolved, with athletes now utilizing complex analytics to inform their equipment and conditioning choices.

51. In the 2010s, teams began using biomechanical research to inform equipment design aimed at enhancing player safety.

52. The development of grass materials has improved player safety by providing a more natural feel underfoot.

53. Specialized lifting equipment in team facilities enhances player strength and conditioning.

54. All helmets must meet specific safety criteria established by the National Operating Committee on Standards for Athletic Equipment (NOCSAE).

55. Many athletes now wear "smart" wristbands to monitor heart rates and exertion levels during games.

56. Modern grip textures used in football manufacturing enhance throwing accuracy and control.

57. The trend towards lightweight helmets has made them easier for athletes to wear without sacrificing protection.

58. Teams routinely test all equipment before each season to ensure compliance with league standards

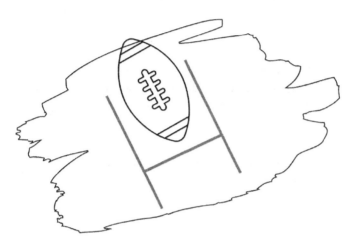

59. Many teams employ full-time staff dedicated exclusively to player safety and equipment innovation.

60. The growing demand for performance apparel has driven innovations in thermal-regulating and moisture-wicking fabrics.

61. Players now use pneumatic compression devices for post-game recovery.

62. The NFL uses a range of data collection technologies to monitor equipment performance and safety.

63. Uniforms made with antimicrobial components help prevent bacterial growth and odor.

64. Teams increasingly seek customized equipment for players based on position, playing style, and body type.

65. The NFL has increasingly adopted virtual fittings for customized equipment, offering improved comfort and performance.

66. Players typically have their helmets custom-fitted based on their individual head shapes to enhance comfort and safety.

67. The NFL has implemented strict regulations regarding the sale of replica equipment to ensure fan safety and quality.

68. In the 2000s, teams began employing laser measuring technology to optimize equipment fit for individual players.

69. Energy-returning elements in shoes now enhance players' speed and efficiency on the field.

Chapter 12: Famous Coaches and Records

1. Bill Belichick, the head coach of the New England Patriots, is generally regarded as one of the top coaches in NFL history with eight Super Bowl titles-six with the Patriots, two with the New York Giants.

2. Vince Lombardi was the coach of the Green Bay Packers to victories in the first two Super Bowls, after whom the trophy is named.

6. Chuck Noll was the first head coach to win four Super Bowl trophies, guiding the Pittsburgh Steelers to victory in the 1970s.

3. Don Shula holds the NFL's record for most career wins as a head coach, with 347 triumphs.

4. George Halas coached the Chicago Bears and founded the NFL; he won six titles and is credited with developing the modern game.

5. Celebrated for his unique fedora, Tom Landry led the Dallas Cowboys into five Super Bowl trips over 29 seasons.

7. Celebrated for developing the "West Coast offense," a revolutionary approach that emphasizes quick, short passes, is Bill Walsh.

8. Showcasing his adaptability, Joe Gibbs is among the few coaches who have won three Super Bowls with three different quarterbacks.

9. Celebrated for his austere look and motivating approach, Bill Parcells led the New York Giants to two Super Bowl victories.

10. Tony Dungy, the first African American head coach, led the Indianapolis Colts to triumph in 2007, winning a Super Bowl.

11. Mike Tomlin, also with the Pittsburgh Steelers, is the youngest head coach to have claimed a Super Bowl at 36.

12. Jimmy Johnson was known for encouraging team discipline as the Dallas Cowboys guided them to two Super Bowl victories in the 1990s.

13. Tom Coughlin, the New York Giants' head coach, most famously led the team to two Super Bowl victories over the New England Patriots.

14. Marv Levy led the Buffalo Bills to four consecutive Super Bowl trips from 1990 to 1993, even though they did not win any.

15. Celebrated for his measured execution of the "defensive game plan," Bill Belichick makes game-specific adjustments for every opponent.

16. Andy Reid, the Kansas City Chiefs' head coach, has directed his team to multiple postseason trips and is well-known for his innovative offensive plans.

17. Following his coaching of the Green Bay Packers to a title in 1997, Mike Holmgren guided the Seattle Seahawks to the Super Bowl.

18. Lou Holtz, mainly renowned as a college coach, briefly coached the New York Jets and is well-known for his inspiring speeches.

19. Following the Oakland Raiders to a Super Bowl victory, John Madden became a well-known broadcaster and video game star.

20. Bill Cowher led the Pittsburgh Steelers to a Super Bowl over more than 15 seasons and built a reputation for his aggressive sideline style.

21. Among the first African American head coaches in the NFL, Art Shell was inducted into the Pro Football Hall of Fame in 1989.

22. Renowned for his offensive ability, Sean Payton led the New Orleans Saints to their first Super Bowl victory in the 2009 season.

23. Mike Shanahan developed quarterbacks like John Elway and won two Super Bowls with the Denver Broncos.

24. Herm Edwards famously said, "You play to win the game!" during a news conference, which came to be a catchphrase of sorts.

25. Bruce Arians, the Tampa Bay Buccaneers' head coach, is renowned for his "no risk it, no biscuit" offense philosophy.

6. Following a controversial loss, Minnesota Vikings head coach Dennis Green is remembered for his famous remark, "They are who we thought they were!".

7. Paul Brown, the Cleveland Browns' founder, is credited with several concepts including the use of game film for player development.

0. Well-known for his cowboy hat and boots, Bum Phillips led the Houston Oilers to numerous late 1970s playoff trips.

I. Stressing deep passes and generating numerous high-scoring games, Don Coryell was known for his "Air Coryell" approach.

. Originally primarily known for his achievements as a college coach, Nick Saban temporarily coached the Miami Dolphins before returning to collegiate football.

. Jeff Fisher owns the record for most losses by a head coach in NFL history, even he is well-known for his strong defensive quads.

. John Fox helped the Denver Broncos reach the Super Bowl and the Carolina Panthers to make their first appearance.

. Tony Sparano was well-known for focusing on the rushing game, having been the head coach of the Miami Dolphins.

28. Though he failed in the playoffs and adopted the term "Martyball," Marty Schottenheimer is more known for his regular-season success.

29. Former Indianapolis Colts head coach Chuck Pagano battled cancer while serving as coach and came to stand for toughness

34. Considered for his defensive acumen, Ray Rhodes coached the Philadelphia Eagles and the Green Bay Packers.

35. Having won a Super Bowl in 2010, Mike McCarthy, head coach of the Green Bay Packers, is renowned for his quarterback management.

38. Dan Reeves helped the Denver Broncos and Atlanta Falcons reach the Super Bowl throughout his career.

39. After his playing years, Kenny "The Snake" Stabler had a successful coaching career leading Arena Football League teams.

40. Among other duties, Pat Shurmur has coached the New York Giants and Cleveland Browns.

41. Celebrated for his aggressive inspiring style, Hall of Fame linebacker Mike Singletary joined the San Francisco 49ers as head coach.

42. Jim Harbaugh was outstanding in college football, leading the San Francisco 49ers to a Super Bowl appearance before returning to the NFL.

44. Gary Kubiak, Denver Broncos head coach, won Super Bowl 50 showcasing his offensive power.

43. Having led the Chicago Bears and Miami Dolphins, Dave Wannstedt is well-known for stressing player development.

45. Thought of for his intense coaching style, Dick Vermeil led the St. Louis Rams to a Super Bowl victory in 1999.

46. Though his stint was troubled, Les Steckel spent a short time heading the Minnesota Vikings.

47. Renowned for his friendly approach to players, Mike Tomlin has maintained the Steelers' winning culture since 2007.

48. Stressing a strong running game, Chuck Knox guided the Los Angeles Rams and Seattle Seahawks successfully.

49. Wade Phillips, Dallas Cowboys' head coach, is well-known for his defensive skills.

50. Renowned for his calm demeanor, Jim Caldwell led the Indianapolis Colts to a Super Bowl trip in 2010.

51. Steve Mariucci coached the San Francisco 49ers and Detroit Lions, well-known for his offensive creativity.

Skills

52. Head coach for the Indianapolis Colts, Rick Venturi is renowned for his defensive strategies.

53. Lou Saban, twice Buffalo Bills head coach, is credited with developing several Hall of Fame players.

54. Reputed for his disciplined coaching style, Tom Coughlin led the New York Giants to two Super Bowl victories.

55. Rex Ryan, coaching the Buffalo Bills and New York Jets, was well-known for his defensive tactics and approach

56. Long with the Cincinnati Bengals, Marvin Lewis was noted for his player development.

57. Celebrated for his leadership, Baltimore Ravens coach John Harbaugh led the team to a Super Bowl victory in 2013.

58. Lovie Smith became the first African American head coach, guiding the Chicago Bears into Super Bowl XLI.

59. Kevin Stefanski, who took over as head coach for the Cleveland Browns, is well-known for overhauling the team's offense.

60. Former player turned coach Mike Vrabel rose quickly to become head coach of the Tennessee Titans.

61. Head Coach of the Miami Dolphins, Brian Flores drew attention with his defensive strategies and player development.

62. Celebrated for his collegiate football skills, Urban Meyer faced challenges adapting to the NFL with the Jacksonville Jaguars.

63. Head coach of the New York Giants, Joe Judge emphasized accountability and discipline in his approach.

64. Sean McVay replaced the head coach of the Los Angeles Rams early on and quickly raised the club's offensive performance.

65. Known for his outstanding leadership, Ron Rivera led the Carolina Panthers to Super Bowl 50.

66. Although largely connected with basketball, Pat Riley briefly coached football in college before focusing on basketball.

67. Dave Campo, a defensive coaching guru, served as the head coach for the Dallas Cowboys.

68. Just as famously as John Madden's coaching career is his impact on football video games and television.

69. Perry Fewell has been a defensive coordinator and temporary head coach for the New York Giants.

70. Brian Kelly, largely a collegiate coach, had a great career at Notre Dame and was hired as head coach of the LSU Tigers football team.

71. Renowned for his innovative offensive strategies, Mike McDaniel is the head coach of the Miami Dolphins.

Chapter 13: NFL Controversies

1. The "Tuck Rule" controversy first arose during the 2001 AFC Divisional Playoff when Tom Brady's fumble was ruled an incomplete pass, allowing the Patriots to triumph against the Oakland Raiders.

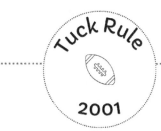

Tuck Rule

2001

2. During the 1982 NFL strike, three games with substitute players attracted criticism from players and fans, sparking debate.

3. The 1972 "Immaculate Reception," in which Franco Harris grabbed a deflected pass for a score, remains one of the most contentious events in NFL history.

7. The "BountyGate" scandal involving the New Orleans Saints focused on players being incentivized to injure opponents.

4. Allegations of deflated footballs led to the "Deflategate" issue involving the Patriots in 2015 as they advanced to the AFC Championship Game.

5. The controversial no-call against the New Orleans Saints in the 2019 NFC Championship Game versus the Los Angeles Rams led to extensive criticism.

6. The NFL's handling of player demonstrations during the national anthem, particularly during the 2016 season, generated significant debate and controversy.

8. Jerry Rice's "fumble" in Super Bowl XXIII produced a controversial ruling that some argued could have affected the game's outcome.

9. The Tennessee Titans' 2000 "Music City Miracle" win against the Buffalo Bills, featuring a last-second lateral, raised questions regarding whether the lateral was a forward pass.

10. The legitimacy of the "Hail Mary" pass Roger Staubach threw against the Minnesota Vikings in 1975 is hotly contested.

11. Concerns arose in 2018 over how the NFL's new helmet contact rules would impact tackling, leading to criticism from players.

12. The "Desmond Howard Touchdown" in Super Bowl XXXI remains a memorable moment, though there are minor debates among fans about his field position.

13. The "Fail Mary" game between the Green Bay Packers and Seattle Seahawks culminated in a controversial touchdown decision, highlighting the 2012 replacement referee issues.

14. The "Kaepernick Effect" refers to the impact of Colin Kaepernick's protest against racial inequity, which sparked significant debate and led to repercussions.

15. Due to COVID-19 regulations, the NFL relocated the 2021 Pro Bowl from Florida to Las Vegas, sparking debates about spectator attendance and player safety.

16. Ongoing discussions about player safety and concussions have resulted in multiple lawsuits against the NFL, especially regarding rules and protocol.

17. Debate continues over the "Roughing the Passer" penalty, with critics arguing the rules negatively impact the game and are too strict.

18. Widespread coach and fan dissatisfaction with the "Pass Interference Challenge" rule in 2019 led to major criticism about inconsistent officiating.

19. The NFL's decision to hold the 2020 Draft virtually amid the pandemic spurred debates over the event's accessibility.

20. Renaming the Washington Redskins to the "Washington Football Team" attracted varied reactions from players and fans, highlighting discussions on cultural sensitivity.

21. Particularly in the Ray Rice case, the NFL faced strong criticism for its disciplinary policies, perceived as lenient regarding domestic violence incidents.

22. Comments by Troy Aikman and Chris Collinsworth about officiating during Super Bowl LV sparked debates over the integrity of officiating.

23. The 2007 "Spygate" scandal involved the New England Patriots obtaining the New York Jets' defensive signals, resulting in fines and the loss of draft picks.

24. The NFL's decision to allow teams to charge for passes during training camps faced criticism from fans who preferred free attendance.

25. Rioting and property damage during the Philadelphia Eagles' 2018 Super Bowl Parade led to condemnation and discussions on fan behavior.

26. Athletes have raised concerns about injury risks associated with artificial turf, fueling ongoing debates over artificial turf versus natural grass fields.

27. The 2010 New Orleans Saints "bounty" program, which paid players to incapacitate opponents, resulted in severe penalties for the franchise.

28. Public criticism and demonstrations have arisen regarding the NFL's handling of health issues among retired players, especially related to head injuries.

29. Known for using complex formations, Cowboys coach Tom Landry's "Landry Shift" drew criticism from rival coaches.

30. Controversy surrounds Aaron Rodgers's "Hail Mary" pass, with some fans disputing its classification and legality.

31. The Miami Dolphins' "Richie Incognito bullying scandal" spurred discussions about mental health and locker room culture in sports.

32. The organization of the 2019 "Kaepernick workout" event led to divided opinions among NFL teams over its structure and purpose.

33. Players and fans criticized the NFL's handling of COVID-19 health protocols and game postponements, raising health concerns.

NFL's
handling
COVID-19

34. Debates arose over the NFL's allowance of alternate uniforms and throwback jerseys, questioning the balance between legacy and commercialism.

35. During the "Eli Manning trade" controversy, he declined to play for the San Diego Chargers, sparking strong reactions from NFL Draft attendees.

36. Ray Lewis's Super Bowl performance stirred discussions, with some believing his legal issues overshadowed his accomplishments.

37. The 2017 "Minnesota Miracle" sparked debates about the officiating and the validity of key plays, particularly regarding the game's final moments.

38. The "Kirk Cousins franchise tag" controversy in 2016 led to extensive discussions about player salaries and team strategies.

39. Reactions were mixed to the NFL's decision to establish a team in London, citing concerns about travel, fan engagement, and competition balance.

40. Player safety and game quality concerns have led to criticism of the "Thursday Night Football" schedule.

41. The NFL's "diverse hiring program" initiative, aimed at increasing minority coaching representation, has prompted questions about its effectiveness.

42. The Cleveland Browns' 0-16 season drew criticism, with fans questioning both player performance and management decisions.

43. The NFL's enforcement of penalties on certain touchdown celebrations has sparked debates over players' rights to self-expression.

44. Brief bans on Rob Gronkowski's "Gronk spike" celebration sparked discussions among fans who view it as integral to his persona.

45. Cris Carter's controversial advice about athletes having a "fall guy" for off-field issues raised ethical questions and faced backlash.

46. The 2019 rule change to "Defensive Pass Interference" drew criticism, with opponents questioning its effect on gameplay.

47. The 2007 "Michael Vick dogfighting scandal" drew condemnation and raised ethical questions about athlete conduct.

48. The NFL's handling of player injuries —particularly concussions—has come under scrutiny, with many considering it inadequate.

49. Renaming the Washington Redskins ignited debates, reflecting broader societal discussions on race and cultural sensitivity.

50. The Tampa Bay Buccaneers' 2003 Super Bowl victory prompted discussions about the team's remarkable transformation to success.

51. Philadelphia Eagles' "quarterback controversy" in 2017 fueled debates over team dynamics and the roles of players.

52. Media scrutiny over player suspensions often centered on cases like the "Greg Hardy domestic violence case."

53. The vagueness of "defensive holding and illegal contact" rules has made them subjects of intense debate due to inconsistent implementation.

54. The NFL's partnerships with gambling companies have raised ethical concerns over player integrity and fan trust.

55. The NFL's growing focus on commercial partnerships and sponsorships has led some fans to question the game's integrity.

56. The "Dez Bryant catch" in the 2014 playoffs raised questions about the NFL's controversial "catch rule."

57. The "Tony Romo injury controversy" raised debates on the role of backup quarterbacks and management's handling of injured players.

58. The "2019 NFL anthem protests" generated significant attention and sparked debates over league policies and player rights.

59. The "College Football Transfer Portal" has influenced discussions on player rights and their implications for academic institutions.

60. The moniker "America's Team" for the Cowboys has drawn criticism, with some fans feeling it reflects media bias.

61. Discussions on team management arose following the "Brett Favre retirement saga" and his eventual return to the league.

62. The NFL's investigation into the "New England Patriots' air pressure scandal" sparked questions about competitive integrity.

63. Supporters of the "Coaches Challenge" rule have raised debates about its implementation and whether it enhances gameplay fairness.

64. The NFL's concussion protocol transparency and effectiveness have been criticized by both players and fans.

65. Off-field conflicts and team chemistry issues in the "Antonio Brown story" led to discussions about mental health in professional sports.

66. Critics of the Washington Football Team's logo change highlighted branding issues and concerns over team identity.

67. The Pro Bowl selection process has drawn criticism, with many arguing it favors popularity over player quality.

68. The NFL's decision to host the 2021 Draft in Cleveland led to debates over the event location and planning.

69. A missed call against the Seahawks during Super Bowl XL raised questions about officiating ethics and fairness.

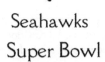

Seahawks
Super Bowl

Chapter 14: NFL Stadiums and Game-day Traditions

1. Lambeau Field, home of the Green Bay Packers, is famous for the "Lambeau Leap," where players jump into the stands to celebrate touchdowns with fans.

2. The Dallas Cowboys' AT&T Stadium features one of the world's largest high-definition video boards, stretching over 60 yards.

3. The Seattle Seahawks' Lumen Field is known for its deafening crowd noise, which has caused multiple false starts for visiting teams.

4. Allegiant Stadium, home of the Las Vegas Raiders, boasts a torch in honor of the late Raiders owner Al Davis.

5. The Buffalo Bills' Highmark Stadium hosts the unique "Shout!" song tradition, where fans sing and dance after every Bills score.

6. The Tennessee Titans' Nissan Stadium is located by the Cumberland River, allowing fans to walk from downtown Nashville via a pedestrian bridge.

7. SoFi Stadium in Los Angeles, shared by the Rams and Chargers, is the most expensive stadium ever built, costing around $5 billion.

8. The Chicago Bears' Soldier Field is the oldest stadium currently in the NFL, having originally opened in 1924.

9. Arrowhead Stadium in Kansas City holds the Guinness World Record for the loudest crowd noise at an outdoor stadium, reaching 142.2 decibels.

10. U.S. Bank Stadium in Minneapolis has a unique transparent roof that allows natural light, simulating an outdoor feel while protecting fans from Minnesota's cold weather.

11. The Green Bay Packers are the only community-owned team in the NFL, with over 360,000 stockholders.

12. State Farm Stadium in Arizona has a fully retractable field that rolls outside to receive sunlight and can roll back in for games.

13. MetLife Stadium, shared by the New York Giants and Jets, is the only stadium home to two NFL teams.

14. Ford Field, home of the Detroit Lions, was constructed within a historic warehouse, incorporating Detroit's industrial heritage into its design.

15. The Baltimore Ravens honor Edgar Allan Poe, a famous Baltimore resident, by having three raven mascots named Edgar, Allan, and Poe.

16. The Denver Broncos' Empower Field at Mile High is located a mile above sea level, impacting the way the ball travels due to the thin air.

17. The New Orleans Saints' Caesars Superdome has hosted more Super Bowls than any other stadium, with a total of seven.

18. Levi's Stadium in San Francisco includes a rooftop garden designed to improve energy efficiency and provide scenic views.

19. Raymond James Stadium in Tampa features a full-scale pirate ship that fires cannons whenever the Buccaneers score.

20. Gillette Stadium in New England has a lighthouse and a foghorn that sounds off to celebrate Patriots' touchdowns.

21. FedEx Field, once the largest stadium in the NFL, had a capacity of 91,000 seats during the early 2000s.

22. AT&T Stadium can expand to hold over 100,000 people by adding standing-room tickets, making it the largest NFL venue by capacity.

23. Hard Rock Stadium in Miami was renovated with a canopy to shield fans from rain, though the field remains uncovered.

24. Mercedes-Benz Stadium in Atlanta has a retractable roof designed to resemble a camera lens.

25. Bank of America Stadium, home of the Carolina Panthers, was one of the first NFL stadiums to adopt fully digital ticketing.

26. The Jacksonville Jaguars' TIAA Bank Field offers fans the unique experience of watching games from a poolside cabana.

27. The San Francisco 49ers' Levi's Stadium is one of the most sustainable stadiums, with solar panels and water recycling systems.

28. Nissan Stadium fans have a unique ritual of gathering on the pedestrian bridge for photos overlooking the stadium.

9. FirstEnergy Stadium, home of the Cleveland Browns, is famous for its "Dawg Pound," a passionate section of fans known for wild costumes and chants.

0. The Philadelphia Eagles' Lincoln Financial Field uses wind turbines and solar panels to generate part of its electricity.

1. The Pittsburgh Steelers' Acrisure Stadium is located at the confluence of Pittsburgh's three rivers, offering scenic views around the venue.

32. Gillette Stadium hosts "The Hall at Patriot Place," a museum dedicated to New England Patriots history.

33. The Raiders' Allegiant Stadium has a field-level club lounge that allows fans to watch the game up close behind the end zone.

34. M&T Bank Stadium in Baltimore became the first stadium to receive LEED Gold certification for environmental sustainability.

35. The Los Angeles Memorial Coliseum has hosted two Olympic Games, along with the Rams, Raiders, and the University of Southern California Trojans.

36. The New York Jets' and Giants' MetLife Stadium can change colors and lighting to match the home team playing that day.

37. The Chicago Bears' Soldier Field is situated near Lake Michigan, providing a distinct setting and often cold, windy conditions.

38. AT&T Stadium has a renowned art collection with over 50 pieces by artists from around the world, making it as much an art gallery as a sports venue.

39. The Minnesota Vikings' Gjallarhorn, a traditional Nordic instrument, is sounded before games, connecting to Minnesota's Scandinavian heritage.

Chapter 15: Fan Culture and Traditions

1. "Swapping jerseys" between supporters of opposing teams helps foster respect and goodwill among rivals after a game.

2. Among Green Bay Packers fans, the "Go Pack Go!" chant is well-known for creating a heated atmosphere at Lambeau Field.

3. Club mascots play an integral role in fan culture, exciting followers and providing entertainment during games.

4. As part of their "Fan Experience," many NFL facilities offer interactive exhibits and meet-and-greets with former players.

5. Fans, especially in Seattle, are often referred to as the "12th man" due to their significant impact on home-field advantage.

6. At some venues, the custom of "ringing the bell" is a unique fan activity where fans physically ring a bell to signal a win.

9. Certain venues celebrate team success by blasting a "victory bell" after a win.

7. Several teams have memorials or statues of legendary athletes, allowing fans to honor their sports heroes.

10. Fans who follow multiple teams across different sports create a diverse range of fan cultures.

8. Celebrated for their extravagant costumes and strong support, Allegiant Stadium in Las Vegas features a "Black Hole" packed with enthusiastic fans.

11. "Face painting" with team colors is a common way for young supporters to express their love and allegiance.

12. The legendary 1924 Notre Dame backfield, known as the "Four Horsemen," remains an iconic part of football lore and connects to NFL fan culture.

13. Victory parades for Super Bowl champions draw thousands of fans and showcase local pride.

14. Face painting often features team colors, symbols, or player numbers as a show of spirit.

15. Fantasy football leagues have gained immense popularity, with millions of participants annually, changing how fans view and engage with games.

16. Several teams have original fight songs to encourage fans to unify during games.

17. The "Trophy Presentation" following a Super Bowl victory is a cherished occasion for fans to celebrate their team's achievements.

18. Many fans follow game-day rituals like wearing lucky items, saying specific prayers, or observing superstitions they believe might influence the game.

19. Interactive video boards at stadiums engage fans by showcasing player highlights, statistics, and contests.

20. Some local businesses offer game-day discounts in areas with NFL teams to encourage fans to support their team while saving money.

21. Many fans participate in fantasy leagues, adding extra excitement and affecting their perceptions of specific players.

22. Many fans take part in "tailgate potlucks," where they bring food to share, strengthening the sense of community.

23. Many NFL facilities feature "fan zones," designated areas for family-friendly interactions and events before a game.

24. Many team supporters participate in charitable events organized by their teams, showcasing a culture of giving back.

25. Many teams honor their top players during home games with "Hall of Fame" tributes.

26. Many teams engage in "community outreach programs," enhancing connections among players, clubs, and local fans.

27. Supporters often create their own catchphrases or sayings to cheer their teams on during games.

28. Fans often design rivalry rituals with specific chants, t-shirts, or themes based on their opponents.

29. Home-field advantage is often attributed to enthusiastic fan support, as boisterous crowds make it challenging for rival teams to communicate.

30. Stadium designs and fan feedback often contribute to creating larger concourses and improved sightlines, enhancing the game-day experience.

31. Supporters frequently create intricate signs to show their support; some even use them to announce players.

32. Many venues host "Fan Appreciation Days," allowing fans to meet players, collect memorabilia, and enjoy a day celebrating their loyalty.

33. Cheerleading became an integral part of NFL games, especially from the 1980s onward, with teams like the Dallas Cowboys leading the trend.

34. Popular tailgate games like cornhole, ladder toss, and beer pong are common at many stadiums.

35. Today's NFL culture is largely commercial, with fans purchasing jerseys, hats, and other merchandise to show loyalty.

36. The "Fan Cam" often features fans during games, providing a way for supporters to engage more and feel connected to the broadcast.

37. Often inspired by historical events or players, the tradition of dressing up for games includes intricate costumes.

38. Access to exclusive events, merchandise, and player meet-and-greets is often granted through official fan clubs established by NFL teams.

39. Especially in the fall and winter, "Sunday is for football" underscores the cultural significance of NFL game days.

Sunday is for football

40. Player entrances are accompanied by dramatic music and pyrotechnics to provide an incredible atmosphere for viewers.

41. Playoff games usually generate more fan enthusiasm as fans prepare for their teams' postseason campaigns.

42. Popular interactive apps enable fans to engage with live game information, make predictions, and share comments.

43. Popular musicians increasingly perform at stadiums before or after games, enhancing the overall fan experience.

44. The iconic "Hail Mary" play has become a cultural benchmark, symbolizing optimism and risk in key moments.

45. Rivalry games attract heightened fan interest, bringing decades-old traditions to the forefront.

46. Season ticket holders often form tight-knit groups and friendships over years of shared game attendance.

47. Several clubs have established "Hall of Fame" areas within their stadiums to honor outstanding players and enhance the fan experience.

48. Fan input often guides team decisions on jersey designs, logo changes, and other branding elements.

49. Singing the national anthem before sporting events is a long-standing tradition, often featuring well-known performers at large-scale events.

Events

50. Social media has transformed fan engagement as platforms like Twitter and Instagram provide new channels for interaction with teams and players.

51. Some clubs celebrate unique traditions, such as "ringing the stadium bells" and tracking scores to energize their followers.

52. .Mystery Bus Tours take fans to unexpected game locations, creating a unique sense of anticipation and excitement.

53. Some fans who travel great distances to follow their teams create a community of dedicated supporters

54. The Pittsburgh Steelers' "Terrible Towel" is a popular ritual, with fans waving it to show team pride.

55. Special promotions encourage fans to dress in costumes or wear festive accessories, especially around holiday-themed events.

56. .Seasonal pop-up stores offer fans unique team merchandise and apparel.

57. Many teams offer stadium tours, giving fans behind-the-scenes access to areas like locker rooms and field levels.

58. Teams that conduct community service events often invite fans to participate, fostering a sense of giving back.

60. Color Rush nights encourage fans to dress in team colors to match the players' all-color uniforms.

60. "Lucky jerseys" are believed to influence team performance, fostering superstitions among supporters.

61. The "Famous Fans" concept features well-known celebrities and personalities attending games, enhancing the atmosphere.

62. Some stadiums offer the "Freeze the Moment" program, enabling fans to capture special events during games with professional photographers.

63. The first home game, or "Inaugural Game," of a team or stadium typically draws high fan interest.

64. Teams often hold "Tailgate of the Year" events where fans showcase their elaborate tailgating setups.

65. The "50-yard line" seating area is one of the most sought-after spots in stadiums, offering the best view for fans.

66. To create a visual effect, fans participate in the wave by raising their arms in sequence across the stadium.

67. The tradition of tailgating before games involves fans gathering in parking lots to grill food, drink, and socialize.

68. Many NFL stadiums offer a "Game Day Experience" with live music, food vendors, and entertainment before kickoff.

69. NFL Draft events are popular fan gatherings, often held at bars or homes where fans celebrate team picks.

70. Throwing T-shirts into the stands during timeouts or halftime is a common tradition, with shirts often featuring team logos or slogans.

71. The home opener, or first game of the season, attracts larger crowds and excitement as fans celebrate a new season.

72. Super Bowl festivities have become a national phenomenon, with fans gathering to watch the championship game regardless of team loyalty.

Chapter 16: NFL Community and Charitable Contributions

1. Through the NFL's "My Cause My Cleats" initiative, players design customized cleats to represent causes they support, bringing awareness to various charities and foundations.

2. The NFL's "Salute to Service" campaign honors military members and veterans, with proceeds from branded merchandise sales going to organizations like the USO and Wounded Warrior Project.

3. Each year, the Walter Payton NFL Man of the Year Award is presented to a player for their volunteer work and impact in their community, one of the league's highest honors.

4. Many NFL players have started their own foundations to support causes close to their hearts, such as J.J. Watt's Foundation, which provides funding for after-school athletic programs.

5. The "NFL Play 60" campaign encourages kids to engage in 60 minutes of physical activity every day, aiming to combat childhood obesity.

6. For over a decade, NFL players have participated in "Breast Cancer Awareness Month" by wearing pink accessories during October games, raising funds for research and awareness.

7. NFL players and teams frequently participate in the "Toys for Tots" program each holiday season, collecting and distributing toys to children in need.

8. In response to COVID-19, the NFL and its players donated millions of dollars to relief efforts, including personal protective equipment and food assistance for frontline workers and affected families.

9. After Hurricane Harvey, Houston Texans' J.J. Watt raised over $41 million for relief efforts, surpassing his initial goal of $200,000.

10. NFL teams often host annual food drives at their stadiums, encouraging fans to bring non-perishable items for local food banks.

11. The league-wide "Crucial Catch" campaign raises awareness about cancer prevention and encourages regular screenings.

12. Seattle Seahawks' Russell Wilson regularly visits the Seattle Children's Hospital, bringing gifts and spending time with young patients.

13. Through the "Huddle for 100" initiative, NFL fans, players, and teams aimed to contribute 100 million minutes of volunteer time to their communities in honor of the NFL's 100th season.

14. Many teams partner with Habitat for Humanity to build homes for families in need, with players often volunteering on-site.

15. Patriots owner Robert Kraft donated $20 million to local Boston charities through the Kraft Family Foundation, supporting education, healthcare, and youth programs

16. Former NFL player Warrick Dunn's "Homes for the Holidays" program has provided over 170 single parents with down-payment assistance for their first homes.

17. The NFL Foundation's "Youth Football Grants" provide funding for local high school and youth football programs to enhance access to the sport.

18. Chicago Bears linebacker Khalil Mack donated $350,000 to his high school's athletic department to support future student-athletes.

19. Through the NFL's "Inspire Change" initiative, teams and players work to address social justice issues, including educational and economic advancement.

20. Buffalo Bills players held a fundraising event to support Western New York children's charities, raising over $1 million in a single night.

21. Former player Anquan Boldin founded the "Players Coalition," a group advocating for social justice and criminal justice reform.

22. The "NFL Green" initiative promotes environmental responsibility through recycling, reforestation projects, and reducing stadium waste.

23. New Orleans Saints' Drew Brees and his wife donated $5 million to Louisiana for COVID-19 relief, supporting meal programs and healthcare workers.

24. The Carolina Panthers' "Keep Pounding" campaign raises funds for cancer research, inspired by former player and coach Sam Mills.

25. Players often participate in annual Thanksgiving community events, distributing meals to families in need and working with food banks.

26. Washington Commanders' Chase Young partnered with Special Olympics, providing resources and support for athletes with disabilities.

27. Arizona Cardinals' Larry Fitzgerald has hosted charity golf tournaments, raising millions of dollars for various causes, including breast cancer awareness.

28. Many NFL teams host "Back to School" events, providing backpacks, school supplies, and educational resources to students.

29. Through "Super Bowl Legacy Grants," the NFL provides funding for community projects in the Super Bowl host city each year.

30. The "NFL Alumni Association" encourages retired players to stay involved in charitable efforts, including youth development and health initiatives.

31. Former NFL quarterback Peyton Manning frequently donates to children's hospitals and opened the Peyton Manning Children's Hospital in Indianapolis.

32. The Los Angeles Rams' "Team Up for Change" initiative brings awareness to issues like racial inequality and social justice through community conversations and events.

33. Cincinnati Bengals' Joe Burrow raised $500,000 for Ohio's Athens County Food Pantry after his Heisman Trophy acceptance speech brought attention to hunger issues.

34. The Denver Broncos support the "Boys & Girls Club of Metro Denver," with team members frequently volunteering their time.

35. The "Touchdown for Tots" program, supported by NFL teams and players, provides holiday gifts for children in foster care.

36. Tampa Bay Buccaneers' Mike Evans founded the Mike Evans Family Foundation to support victims of domestic violence and offer scholarships to low-income students.

37. The San Francisco 49ers host an annual "Holiday Wish Drive" to collect gifts and donations for children in foster care.

38. The NFL Foundation funds "High School Football Kickoff Grants" to help under-resourced schools launch or maintain their football programs.

39. Through "Coach of the Week" programs, teams recognize and support local high school coaches who positively impact their communities.

40. The "NFL Flag" program, sponsored by the NFL Foundation, supports coed flag football leagues, promoting youth fitness and teamwork.

Chapter 17: NFL's Global Influence

1. The first NFL game played outside the United States took place in Canada in 1926 between the New York Yankees and the Los Angeles Wildcats.

2. In 1986, the Chicago Bears and Dallas Cowboys played the first official American Bowl in London's Wembley Stadium.

3. The NFL hosts regular-season games in London as part of the International Series, which began in 2007 with the Giants vs. Dolphins game.

5. The NFL's International Series expanded to Germany in 2022, with the Tampa Bay Buccaneers and Seattle Seahawks playing in Munich.

4. Mexico City hosted its first regular-season NFL game in 2005, with the Arizona Cardinals defeating the San Francisco 49ers in front of 103,467 fans.

6. The London-based NFL games often sell out within minutes, attracting fans from across Europe.

7. The Buffalo Bills played a series of home games in Toronto, Canada, from 2008 to 2013, to expand their fan base.

8. The NFL hosted its first game in China in 2018, though it was only a preseason scrimmage.

9. NFL Europe, a developmental league, ran from 1991 to 2007, producing players like Kurt Warner.

10. In 2016, the NFL hosted its first Pro Bowl a non-U.S. location, held in Hawaii.

12. The NFL's official shop delivers merchandise to over 100 countries worldwide.

11. The Super Bowl is broadcast in over 180 countries and translated into more than 25 languages.

13. The Jacksonville Jaguars committed to playing one "home" game in London annually starting in 2013.

14. NFL players like Odell Beckham Jr. and Tom Brady have large fan followings in countries like Brazil and the U.K.

15. Japan's X-League is a semi-professional football league heavily inspired by the NFL.

16. The NFL collaborated with Tottenham Hotspur to design a stadium specifically equipped for American football games.

17. Canadian fans account for one of the largest international audiences for the NFL, especially supporting teams like the Buffalo Bills.

18. Super Bowl Sunday is considered a major event in countries like Australia, where bars open early to accommodate fans.

19. American football is growing in popularity in China, with the NFL launching programs to teach the sport in schools.

20. The NFL combines held in London have attracted scouts from both American and international leagues.

21. NFL Mexico has a dedicated office that promotes American football and supports a growing fan base.

22. Germany consistently ranks as the country with the highest number of NFL Game Pass subscribers outside North America.

23. In 2017, the Oakland Raiders played the New England Patriots in Mexico City, drawing over 75,000 fans.

24. American football was an official demonstration sport at the 1932 Olympics in Los Angeles.

25. The NFL has a partnership with Disney to broadcast games on ESPN Asia, reaching millions of viewers.

26. The annual NFL Draft has been streamed live in multiple languages, including Spanish and Mandarin.

27. NFL Australia hosts viewing parties for fans to watch games and meet NFL alumni.

28. The first European-born player drafted into the NFL was Bo Eason in 1984.

29. Over 400 million people globally watch the Super Bowl each year, making it one of the most-watched events worldwide.

30. Mexico's national football league is one of the largest outside the U.S., with over 2 million participants.

31. The NFL Foundation has donated millions of dollars to develop football programs in underprivileged regions worldwide.

32. Brazil's São Paulo Spartans, a semi-pro football team, has collaborated with NFL coaches for training sessions.

33. The NFL partnered with the U.K.'s Sky Sports to launch a dedicated NFL channel in 2020.

34. Japan's universities have a thriving football culture, often sending players to NFL scouting programs.

35. NFL alumni often host clinics in Africa to introduce the sport to young athletes.

36. American football is the fastest-growing sport in Australia among women athletes.

37. NFL Germany launched its own TikTok channel in 2021, quickly amassing millions of followers.

38. The NFL organized its first fan festival in Shanghai in 2019, attended by over 10,000 fans.

39. Canadian Football League (CFL) players occasionally transition to the NFL, like Warren Moon and Cameron Wake.

40. NFL broadcasts in Japan date back to the 1970s and remain popular today.

41. London's Wembley Stadium holds the record for hosting the most NFL games outside the U.S.

42. The NFL introduced a rule change in 2018 allowing teams to host more games abroad.

43. NFL fans in Germany launched "Footballerei," a podcast dedicated to NFL commentary in German.

44. The first NFL game in Mexico featured cheerleaders performing a halftime show that included local dance traditions.

45. NFL Canada provides free curriculum resources to teach football skills in schools.

46. South Korea's American Football Association has teams competing nationwide, inspired by the NFL's structure.

47. NFL players like Russell Wilson have appeared in promotional campaigns in the U.K. to boost the league's profile.

48. The NFL plans to expand games into South America, particularly targeting Brazil.

49. American football in Italy dates back to the 1980s, with leagues adopting many NFL rules.

50. NFL Game Pass subscriptions surged in India after promotional campaigns in cricket-dominated markets.

51. The NFL has sponsored flag football programs in over 50 countries.

52. NFL Films has created documentaries for fans in non-English-speaking countries with localized narration.

53. International players like Efe Obada (U.K.) and Jordan Mailata (Australia) have found success in the NFL.

54. The NFL's annual "Fan Mobile Pass" app is available worldwide, making fan interactions borderless.

55. The Super Bowl generates millions of social media impressions from international audiences every year.

56. Spain's amateur football leagues have grown rapidly thanks to NFL influence.

57. The NFL regularly hosts international coaching clinics to train referees and coaches abroad.

58. The first female international NFL player, Morayo Solaja, hailed from the U.K

59. Fans from over 30 countries participate in NFL fantasy football leagues.

60. NFL gear, including jerseys, is among the most purchased sports merchandise in Japan.

61. London-based fan clubs like the "UK Packers" are highly active, organizing trips to NFL games.

62. American football has become increasingly popular in the Philippines due to NFL streaming services.

63. NFL ambassadors visit international schools to teach students the basics of football.

64. NFL Network introduced multilingual commentary in French and Portuguese in 2019.

65. l.Germany's fan base has outpaced the U.K. as the largest in Europe.

66. The NFL actively promotes its Play 60 program internationally to encourage physical activity among children.

67. The NFL created a Spanish-language website to better engage Hispanic fans worldwide.

68. International NFL fan forums are held annually to connect global communities.

69. NFL pre-season games have been played in Ireland, Sweden, and Finland.

70. Super Bowl parties in Canada sometimes rival those in the U.S. for size and enthusiasm.

71. NFL branding appears in international video games like FIFA to attract global audiences.

72. The NFL hosted its first game in Brazil in 2014, a demonstration match in São Paulo

73. NFL academies in the U.K. train young players for possible NFL careers.

74. American football teams in Africa often watch NFL games to study strategies and techniques.

75. The NFL aired its first Japanese-language broadcast of a live game in 2017.

76. Fans in Australia have created "Gridiron Down Under," a community for NFL discussions.

77. Germany's Frankfurt Galaxy was one of the most successful teams in NFL Europe history.

78. NFL-themed pop-up events in Paris have drawn crowds of over 5,000.

79. The NFL launched an Arabic social media campaign in 2020 to engage Middle Eastern fans.

80. The NFL is exploring partnerships with major cricket leagues to promote cross-sport collaboration in India.

Chapter 18: Bizarre Weather Games in NFL History

The "Ice Bowl" of 1967, played between the Packers and Cowboys, had a temperature of -13°F with a wind chill of -48°F, making it the coldest NFL game ever.

The "Fog Bowl" in 1988 saw the Eagles and Bears battling in near-zero visibility due to a dense fog rolling into Soldier Field during the game.

3. The Patriots and Raiders faced off in the infamous "Snow Bowl" in 2001, remembered for the Tuck Rule and blizzard-like conditions.

4. In 1975, the Bengals played the Chargers in a game nicknamed the "Freezer Bowl," with a wind chill of -59°F, the coldest playoff game in NFL history.

The "Monsoon Bowl" of 1997 saw the Chargers and Colts playing in torrential rain, resulting in multiple fumbles and a waterlogged field.

The 2010 Vikings vs. Giants game was moved to Detroit after heavy snow collapsed the roof of the Metrodome in Minnesota.

A 1982 Dolphins vs. Patriots game became known as the "Snowplow Game" after a worker used a snowplow to clear a path for a successful field goal.

8. A "Mud Bowl" between the Dolphins and Jets in 1982 saw the field turn into a swamp due to heavy rain, with players sliding all over.

9. In 2007, the Steelers and Dolphins played in a game where the field was so waterlogged that punts stuck in the mud on landing.

10. The Eagles faced the Lions in a 2013 "Snow Bowl," with snow falling so heavily that it covered the yard markers and slowed gameplay significantly.

11. The "Wind Bowl" of 2008 between the Bills and Patriots saw gusts of over 50 mph, making passing nearly impossible.

12. A lightning storm in 2013 delayed a Ravens vs. Broncos game for over an hour, one of the longest weather delays in NFL history.

13. In 2016, Hurricane Matthew forced the postponement of a Dolphins vs. Titans game in Florida due to flooding concerns.

14. The Jets and Bills played a 2009 game during a blizzard, with snowdrifts piling up around the sidelines.

15. During a 1983 Packers game, wind gusts of 70 mph led to goalposts bending and requiring reinforcement mid-game.

16. The Cowboys and Eagles played in a "Heat Bowl" in 1977, with on-field temperatures exceeding 120°F.

17. In 1984, a game between the Seahawks and Chiefs featured torrential rain and winds strong enough to blow the football during kickoffs.

18. The "Dust Bowl" of 2005 saw the Cardinals and Cowboys playing amid dust storms in Arizona, reducing visibility.

Dust Bowl

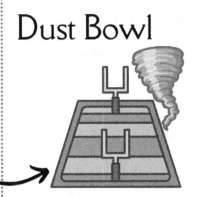

19. A 1970 game between the Browns and Vikings was played during a heavy hailstorm, with marble-sized hail pelting players.

20. The Saints and Bengals played in an "Air Bowl" in 1980, where smog and smoke from nearby wildfires filled the stadium.

21. The 2018 Rams vs. Chiefs game was moved from Mexico City to Los Angeles due to poor field conditions after heavy rain.

22. In 1993, a Packers game was halted briefly due to a tornado warning near the stadium.

23. The "Thunderstorm Game" in 2013 between the Dolphins and Buccaneers had multiple weather delays due to lightning strikes

24. In 2010, a Texans game was postponed due to record flooding in Houston that made the stadium inaccessible.

25. A 2018 Jets vs. Bills game saw freezing rain coat players and fans in ice throughout the game.

26. In 2004, a Colts game had temperatures so cold that Gatorade froze on the sidelines.

27. The "Tropical Storm Bowl" in 2008 between the Panthers and Buccaneers featured driving rain and gusting winds from Hurricane Ike.

28. A 1979 Raiders vs. Broncos game became the "Sleet Bowl," with a mix of rain and snow making the field a skating rink.

29. In 1987, the Vikings and Bears played during freezing drizzle, leading to constant slipping and dropped passes.

30. A 2002 Titans game experienced 60 mph wind gusts, resulting in missed field goals and poor passing.

31. A 1978 Steelers game featured snow drifts on the field so high they obscured players' legs from view.

37. A Buffalo Bills fan proposed to his girlfriend while jumping through a table during a tailgate.

38. "Jets Batman" is a New York Jets superfan who attends games dressed in a Batman costume in team colors.

32. The "Sun Bowl" of 2003 between the Cardinals and Seahawks had on-field temperatures over 110°F.

33. A 1985 game between the Giants and 49ers was dubbed the "Rain Bowl" after four inches of rain fell during the game.

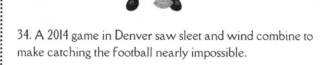

34. A 2014 game in Denver saw sleet and wind combine to make catching the football nearly impossible.

35. The 2012 Ravens vs. Steelers game experienced icy rain that made the field resemble a skating rink.

36. In 1999, a Dolphins game was interrupted by a lightning strike hitting near the stadium.

37. The "Hurricane Bowl" of 1974 saw the Dolphins and Buccaneers playing in hurricane-force winds

38. A Browns vs. Bengals game in 2010 became the "Fog Bowl II" due to thick fog rolling in from Lake Erie.

39. In 2015, a Broncos game saw hail covering the field, leading to slippery conditions.

40. A 2001 Patriots game had players struggling to see through a blizzard with near-zero visibility.

41. The Bears and Packers played in a 1960 "Flood Bowl," where water pooled ankle-deep on the field.

42. In 1980, a Rams game was delayed by an earthquake near the stadium.

43. A 1995 Chiefs game was called the "Cold Snap Game," with wind chills hitting -30°F.

44. The "Rain Curtain" in 2011 saw the Seahawks and Ravens playing during a torrential downpour in Seattle.

47. The "Swamp Bowl" of 1988 between the Saints and 49ers had players covered in mud from head to toe.

48. In 2002, the Cardinals played a game under 100-degree heat during an Arizona heatwave.

45. A 2003 Lions vs. Packers game had snow so deep that players left visible trenches in their wake.

49. A 1990 Steelers game saw heavy fog mixed with snow, reducing visibility for fans and players.

46. A 2016 Cowboys game had gale-force winds affecting punts and passes.

50. The 2014 "Polar Vortex Game" between the Packers and Bears had temperatures of -15°F at kickoff.

51. In 1971, the Colts played during a rainstorm that flooded the field to shin height.

52. A 2017 Jaguars vs. Browns game featured swirling snow and ice pellets.

53. The "Windstorm Game" of 1983 between the Cowboys and Oilers saw wind blowing footballs off tee stands.

54. A 2006 Seahawks game saw sleet and freezing rain disrupt the second half.

55. The "Heat Bowl II" of 1985 between the Dolphins and Raiders featured 115°F temperatures on the field.

56.In 1979, the Patriots played during a snowstorm so intense that the field required plowing between plays.

57. A 2011 49ers game had strong winds cause scoreboard panels to detach and blow onto the field.

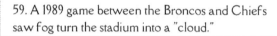

58. The "Frost Bowl" in 1996 between the Jets and Bills had frost forming on helmets during the game.

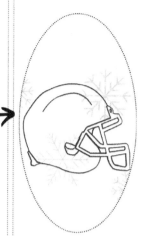

59. A 1989 game between the Broncos and Chiefs saw fog turn the stadium into a "cloud."

60. A 2015 Patriots game experienced hail the size of golf balls hitting the field.

61. The "Ice Rink Game" of 1998 had the Packers and Lions slipping constantly due to icy rain.

62. A 2007 Steelers game had mud so thick that running plays were almost impossible.

63. In 2013, the Seahawks played during a thunderstorm that caused multiple delays.

64. A 1982 game between the Dolphins and Patriots was nicknamed the "Rain Bowl II" after torrential downpours.

65. The "Foggy Night Game" in 1990 between the Eagles and Bears saw fans unable to see the field.

66. A 1994 Jets game featured lightning striking the scoreboard mid-game.

67. The "Flood Game" of 2015 between the Texans and Titans had water pooling knee-deep around the field.

68. A 2019 game between the Cowboys and Eagles had players slipping due to ice forming in unexpected cold.

69. The "Slush Bowl" in 1987 had the Bills and Patriots playing on a partially frozen field.

70. A 2008 Browns game was delayed due to tornado warnings in the area.

71. The "Icy Wind Bowl" of 1980 between the Vikings and Packers had wind chills of -20°F.

72. A 2011 Ravens game had snow falling so fast that visibility disappeared entirely by halftime.

74. A 2005 Seahawks game featured hail turning the field white for most of the game.

73. The "Cold Rain Bowl" of 2014 saw the Patriots and Broncos battling freezing rain throughout.

75. The "Lightning Bowl" of 1991 saw the Saints and Falcons dealing with lightning that forced fans to evacuate.

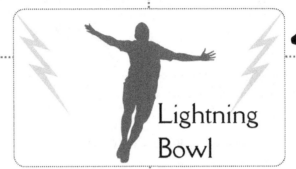

Lightning Bowl

76. A 2000 Packers game had a sudden downpour create a "waterfall" effect over the stands.

79. The "Gale Bowl" of 1996 had winds so strong that kicks went backward mid-air.

77. The "Hot Turf Bowl" in 1984 between the Lions and Dolphins had field temperatures of 135°F.

80. A 2019 Browns game had such heavy rain that the ball splashed every time it hit the ground.

78. A 1992 Eagles game featured freezing fog that coated the players' helmets and uniforms in ice.

Chapter 19: NFL Superfans and Their Stories

1. "Fireman Ed" is a legendary New York Jets fan known for leading the J-E-T-S chants at games since the 1980s.

2. Kansas City Chiefs fans hold the Guinness World Record for the loudest crowd noise in a stadium, recorded at 142.2 decibels in Arrowhead Stadium in 2014.

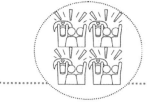

142.2 decibels

3. The "Dawg Pound," a section for Cleveland Browns superfans, was created in the 1980s by fans dressed as dogs to intimidate opponents.

4. "Viking World Order" is a fan group of die-hard Minnesota Vikings supporters who don Viking costumes at every game.

5. .Buffalo Bills fans, also known as "Bills Mafia," are famous for their tailgate antics, including smashing through tables.

6. "Barrel Man," a Denver Broncos superfan, attended games wearing only a barrel and a cowboy hat in freezing weather for over 30 years.

7. Green Bay Packers fans are famously known as "Cheeseheads," a term reclaimed after being used as an insult by rival fans.

8. "Sea Gals," a group of Seattle Seahawks superfans, are known for organizing massive charity events and boosting team spirit.

9. "Big Nasty," a Tampa Bay Buccaneers superfan, is known for his elaborate pirate-themed costume and has won multiple NFL fan awards.

10. "Raider Nation" boasts some of the most intimidating fans, with elaborate costumes like Darth Vader masks and skull face paint.

11. A Dallas Cowboys fan spent over $1 million turning his home into a Cowboys-themed museum.

12. "Captain Dee-Fense," a Baltimore Ravens superfan, is famous for his superhero-like costume and rallying cries during games.

13. The Philadelphia Eagles have some of the most passionate fans, once booing Santa Claus during a halftime show in 1968.

14. A San Francisco 49ers superfan created a replica of the Vince Lombardi Trophy entirely out of Legos.

15. "The Hogettes," a group of Washington Commanders superfans, became famous for wearing pig snouts and dresses to games.

16. A die-hard Chicago Bears fan owns a collection of memorabilia dating back to the team's founding in 1920.

17. "License Plate Guy," a New York Giants superfan, wears a chain of New York license plates representing key moments in team history.

18. A fan of the New Orleans Saints created a golden Superdome replica entirely out of Mardi Gras beads.

19. Las Vegas Raiders superfans often get matching tattoos to commemorate attending games together.

20. "Birdman," a die-hard Atlanta Falcons fan, attends games dressed as a red bird, complete with feathered wings.

21. Fans of the Miami Dolphins, called the "Dolfans," have an official fan club with over 30,000 members worldwide.

22. A New England Patriots fan holds the record for attending every game, home and away, for over 25 years.

23. Pittsburgh Steelers fans are known for waving "Terrible Towels," a tradition started by broadcaster Myron Cope in 1975.

24. A Jacksonville Jaguars fan created a life-sized jaguar sculpture out of recycled materials to display during games.

25. Tennessee Titans superfans often dress as Greek gods, drawing inspiration from the team's name.

26. Detroit Lions fans once organized a "fan walkout" during a game in protest of poor team management.

27. An Arizona Cardinals fan built a mini replica of the State Farm Stadium in his backyard for game-day parties.

28. "The Whistler," a Seattle Seahawks superfan, became famous for his ability to whistle loud enough to distract opponents.

29. Indianapolis Colts fans created a giant horseshoe mosaic made from autographed memorabilia.

30. Houston Texans fans organize an annual chili cook-off to kick off the season in true Texas style.

31. "The Chief," a Kansas City Chiefs fan, wears a full Native American headdress to games, becoming a team icon.

32. A Las Vegas Raiders fan holds the Guinness World Record for the most team tattoos, with over 100.

33. An NFL fan from Germany flies to the U.S. every year to attend games for his favorite team, the Green Bay Packers.

34. A Carolina Panthers superfan dressed as a black panther leads tailgate parades before games.

37. A Buffalo Bills fan proposed to his girlfriend while jumping through a table during a tailgate.

38. "Jets Batman" is a New York Jets superfan who attends games dressed in a Batman costume in team colors.

35. A Cincinnati Bengals fan created a shrine dedicated to the team in his basement, including a mural of the team's mascot.

36. Dallas Cowboys fans hold an annual "Blue and Silver Ball" to celebrate their team.

39. A San Francisco 49ers fan created a functioning gold 49ers helmet made entirely of chocolate.

40. An Oakland Raiders superfan converted his car into a "Raider-Mobile," complete with skull decorations and team colors.

41. The Cleveland Browns have a cemetery-themed tailgate spot, symbolizing their "die-hard" loyalty.

42. A Philadelphia Eagles fan owns a vintage jersey from every year since the team's founding in 1933.

43. A Green Bay Packers fan built a cheese-shaped mailbox in honor of the team.

44. An Arizona Cardinals fan's wedding featured team-themed decorations and jerseys for the entire bridal party.

45. "The Saint," a New Orleans Saints fan, attends games dressed in a priest's outfit to "bless" the team.

46. "Steely McBeam," the Pittsburgh Steelers mascot, was named through a fan contest.

47. Las Vegas Raiders fans have organized charity events that raised over $1 million in the past decade.

48. A Minnesota Vikings fan crafted a fully functional Viking ship float for tailgate parties.

49. "Cowboy Ken," a Dallas Cowboys superfan, turned his home into a fully Cowboys-themed museum.

50. A Denver Broncos fan created a Broncos-themed roller coaster in his backyard.

51. The "Big Cat Crew" is a fan group of Carolina Panthers enthusiasts who tailgate in full leopard-print outfits.

52. Kansas City Chiefs fans once organized a world record attempt for the largest simultaneous "tomahawk chop."

53. An Eagles fan turned his basement into a recreation of Lincoln Financial Field.

54. Pittsburgh Steelers fans are known to travel so well that stadiums often have more Steelers fans than home-team fans.

55. A Seattle Seahawks fan made a life-sized totem pole featuring famous players.

56. The "Cheesehead Priest," a Green Bay Packers superfan, incorporates game-day prayers into his sermons.

57. "Sarge," a Washington Commanders superfan, leads chants in a military uniform at every home game.

58. A Chicago Bears fan carved a life-sized bear out of wood to display at tailgates.

59. A Miami Dolphins fan's custom tailgate bus features a working mini pool on the roof.

60. Detroit Lions fans created a giant papier-mâché lion that roars when the team scores.

61. "Vikings Man," a Minnesota Vikings superfan, wears a full suit of armor to every game.

62. A Green Bay Packers fan holds the record for the largest collection of Packers bobbleheads.

63. An Atlanta Falcons fan built a 20-foot inflatable falcon for tailgates.

64. A Dallas Cowboys fan recreated iconic moments in team history using Legos.

65. The "Bird Gang," Arizona Cardinals fans, is known for its loud chants and organized road trips.

66. A Buffalo Bills fan designed a Bills-themed "tiny house" for tailgates.

67. A Philadelphia Eagles fan once walked 100 miles to attend a game.

68. A Pittsburgh Steelers fan crafted a massive Terrible Towel mural out of mini towels.

69. The Jacksonville Jaguars' "Roaring Rowdies" fan group hosts pregame pep rallies in full jungle-themed gear.

70. An Indianapolis Colts fan's tattoo of the team's logo won a national contest for NFL tattoos.

71. A Cleveland Browns fan built a working football cannon for pregame celebrations.

72. "Captain Colt," an Indianapolis Colts superfan, dresses in a blue superhero costume for every game.

73. A San Francisco 49ers fan holds the record for the largest collection of autographed team helmets.

74. The "Bolt Brigade," Los Angeles Chargers fans, is known for its lightning-themed outfits.

75. A Miami Dolphins fan turned his boat into a floating tailgate for home games.

76. A Seattle Seahawks fan crafted a giant hawk sculpture made of recycled metal.

77. A Las Vegas Raiders fan's wedding featured guests in full Raider costumes.

78. The Kansas City Chiefs "Kingdom Choir" sings team anthems at every home game.

79. A Green Bay Packers fan built a life-sized snow sculpture of Lambeau Field in his yard.

80. The Dallas Cowboys fan club in Japan boasts over 10,000 members, making it one of the largest international fan clubs.

Chapter 20: NFL Behind the Scenes

1. NFL referees are required to attend an annual rules seminar and pass a written test before each season.

2. The average NFL game involves over 300 people working behind the scenes, from camera operators to medical staff.

3. It takes approximately 1,000 people to produce the Super Bowl, including production crew, stadium staff, and performers.

4. NFL referees use wireless headsets to communicate with each other during games.

5. Each NFL game requires at least 36 footballs, which are inspected and approved by officials before kickoff.

6. NFL game balls are hand-stitched in a factory in Ada, Ohio, by Wilson Sporting Goods.

7. The instant replay system requires a dedicated team of operators and technicians to ensure smooth reviews.

8. NFL groundskeepers often spend weeks preparing fields for games, especially during winter months.

9. Every NFL stadium has a team of weather experts to monitor game-day conditions.

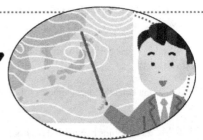

10. The chains used to measure first downs are exactly 10 yards long, and each set includes a backup chain.

11. Sideline markers, pylons, and goalpost padding must meet strict NFL safety standards.

12. NFL medical teams include orthopedic surgeons, trainers, and independent concussion specialists

13. The NFL uses tracking chips in player pads to collect real-time data on speed and movement during games.

14. The headsets used by coaches to communicate with quarterbacks are encrypted to prevent interception.

15. NFL teams employ dedicated statisticians who log every play in real time.

16. Stadium announcers are provided a script by the NFL, ensuring consistency across all games.

7. NFL locker rooms are stocked with a team's preferred brand of snacks, drinks, and recovery products.

8. The NFL uses custom-designed camera rigs, like the SkyCam, to provide aerial views of the field.

19. Ball boys and girls are tasked with keeping game balls warm and dry in bad weather.

20. NFL referees have an official uniform supplier, and their gear is specially designed for visibility.

---

1. Each NFL team has an equipment manager responsible for maintaining helmets, jerseys, and pads.

2. The league employs a "uniform inspector" for each game to ensure players adhere to dress code rules.

23. Sound engineers adjust crowd noise levels for broadcasts to capture the atmosphere without overwhelming viewers.

24. NFL coaches receive updated game statistics on tablets during games, replacing traditional playbooks.

---

5. Game-day security includes plainclothes officers stationed throughout stadiums.

6. NFL stadiums must have backup power generators to prevent blackouts during games.

7. The coin used for the opening toss is often custom-made for each game.

---

8. TV networks use a dedicated "yellow line operator" to add the first down marker on broadcasts.

9. NFL teams travel with chefs to prepare team meals tailored to players' dietary needs.

10. Pregame pyrotechnic displays are coordinated by licensed explosives experts.

31. Stadium DJs are responsible for choosing music that adheres to NFL guidelines for appropriateness.

32. NFL halftime shows are rehearsed multiple times to ensure precise timing.

33. Stadium concession workers often undergo game-day training to manage high-volume crowds.

34. The NFL's official football supplier has been making game balls since 1941.

35. The surface of every NFL field is inspected by officials before games for potential hazards.

36. The NFL uses a "K-ball," a special kicking football, which is different from the game-used balls.

37. The "spotters" in the press box alert officials to potential player injuries during games.

38. Sideline camera operators wear helmets for safety during high-action plays.

39. Each NFL team employs nutritionists to develop player-specific meal plans.

40. The NFL mandates that fields be painted with non-toxic, eco-friendly paint.

41. Backup referees are present at every game in case of injuries to on-field officials.

42. NFL play clocks are operated manually to ensure accuracy in case of technical errors.

43. The NFL has a team of rule analysts in New York monitoring every game in real time.

44. Custom-built trucks parked outside stadiums manage instant replays and broadcast feeds.

45. The halftime intermission for Super Bowl games is longer to accommodate elaborate performances.

46. Each NFL team has a travel coordinator to handle transportation and lodging logistics.

47. The sideline injury tent provides privacy for quick medical evaluations during games.

48. Broadcast teams use specialized microphones to capture the sound of tackles and hits.

49. Every NFL stadium is equipped with a high-speed internet network for officials and media.

50. Head coaches have a direct communication line to their team's spotters in the press box.

51. Each NFL game is overseen by a "game-day observer" who ensures league policies are followed.

52. The NFL has specific standards for how grass fields should be cut and maintained.

53. Referees undergo fitness tests before each season to ensure they can keep up with the pace of play.

54. NFL teams employ video analysts who review footage of opponents to strategize for upcoming games.

55. Groundskeepers use heaters to prevent frozen turf in cold-weather stadiums.

56. Sideline medical carts are equipped with emergency supplies, including defibrillators.

57. The NFL mandates the use of synthetic turf for specific stadiums to reduce maintenance costs.

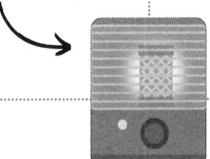

58. All NFL fields must meet strict lighting requirements for TV broadcasts.

59. Camera operators use gyro-stabilized mounts to ensure smooth footage during action shots.

60. The NFL provides each team with 12 tablets loaded with official game footage for in-game analysis.

61. The league has a centralized review center in New York City for instant replay decisions.

62. NFL referees communicate play reviews to the stadium audience via wireless microphones.

63. Teams employ psychologists to support players' mental health and performance.

64. The NFL mandates a specific Gatorade color for sideline coolers to maintain brand consistency.

65. Every NFL stadium has a designated room for drug testing players post-game.

66. Coaches receive laminated play sheets with color-coded plays for quick reference.

67. Sideline reporters are given real-time injury updates from team medical staff.

68. The NFL tests game balls at halftime to ensure they remain inflated within regulation.

69. "Water engineers" maintain hydration systems for players during games.

70. NFL referees are mic'd up, allowing their calls and discussions to be broadcast to viewers.

71. The stadium clock is synchronized with a central NFL timer to ensure accuracy.

72. Game-day volunteers assist with tasks like distributing programs and managing VIP guests.

73. NFL trainers use portable cryotherapy devices for on-the-spot player recovery.

74. Each team has a "field coordinator" responsible for sideline operations during games.

75. NFL cameras use 8K resolution to capture ultra-clear replays and highlights.

76. The NFL uses drones for aerial footage in select stadiums with open roofs.

77. Post-game cleanup crews work overnight to prepare stadiums for the next event.

78. NFL teams provide custom earplugs for players to protect against loud stadium noise.

79. Instant replay booths on the sideline are shielded from crowd noise to avoid distractions.

80. NFL equipment managers ensure each player's gear is cleaned, sanitized, and ready before every game.

Leave Your Feedback on Amazon

Please think about leaving some feedback via a review on Amazon.

It may only take a moment, but it really does mean the world for small publishers like us :)

Parents, Don't Forget Your Free Gifts!

Simply visit **haydenfoxmedia.com** to receive the following:

- *1000 Conversation Starters the Whole Family Will Love*

- *100 Fun Screen-Free Activity Ideas to Enjoy Together as a Family*

(you can also scan this QR code)

Made in the USA
Monee, IL
17 December 2024